D0732619

A Simple Guide to Luke

Paul J. McCarren, SJ

A SHEED & WARD BOOK

ROWMAN & LITTLEFIELD PUBLISHERS, INC.
Lanham • Boulder • New York • Toronto • Plymouth, UK

A Sheed & Ward Book

Published by Rowman & Littlefield Publishers, Inc.
A wholly owned subsidiary of The Rowman & Littlefield Publishing Group, Inc.
4501 Forbes Boulevard, Suite 200, Lanham, Maryland 20706
www.rowman.com

10 Thornbury Road, Plymouth PL6 7PY, United Kingdom

British Library Cataloguing in Publication Information Available

Library of Congress Cataloging-in-Publication Data

McCarren, Paul J., 1943–
A simple guide to Luke / Paul J. Mccarren.
p. cm.
"A Sheed & Ward book."
Includes index.
ISBN 978-1-4422-1881-9 (cloth : alk. paper)—ISBN 978-1-4422-1882-6 (pbk. : alk. paper)—ISBN 978-1-4422-1883-3 (electronic)
1. Bible. N.T. Luke—Commentaries. I. Title.
BS2595.53.M34 2013
226.4'077—dc23
2012031567

Printed in the United States of America

Contents

Introduction

Why I Needed a Simple Guide to the Gospels

It took me a long time to hear what the Gospels say. Luckily, I spent much of that time with the Jesuits, an organization that is patient with slow learners. Like all the other religious orders in the Catholic Church, the Jesuits attempt to respond to Jesus' command in the Gospels to spread the Good News. So Jesuits are required to take time learning what's proclaimed in the Good News. One method used in this learning process is the Spiritual Exercises of Ignatius Loyola. Most of those exercises are contemplations of Gospel scenes that are undertaken with the help of a director, just as physical exercises are often done with the help of a trainer. Jesuits go through these exercises at least twice. I did the Spiritual Exercises as a Jesuit novice; but when I did them again years later, I was shocked to discover I had no idea what I was doing.

The shock hit me late one afternoon as I read to my director a description of how the exercises had gone that day. As I read, he began to cough and clear his throat. He reached for a tissue and said, "Sorry; please excuse me. I've sometimes cried while listening to a write-up, but I've never laughed so hard." My look must have said, "What's so funny?" So he asked me to listen to what I'd been writing. After he read from notes he'd taken on my write-ups, he said, "Notice how you're picturing Jesus." I'd been imagining Jesus acting as a stern teacher who could barely control his impatience with people's slowness to understand his message. Over and over in my prayers I had seen Jesus as a man who was quick to find fault with the mistakes made by his followers. After asking me to notice that this image wasn't very appealing, my director reminded me that the Gospels describe someone quite different from the Jesus I'd imagined. They tell us, for instance, that many people found Jesus immensely attractive. Some of them even dropped everything to follow him. I had missed this simple fact. How was that possible?

At some point in my life I had slipped into the assumption that, because the Gospels describe a God who is infinite, it must be infinitely difficult to relate to him. The logic of that assumption seemed as obvious as the fact that because the theories of modern physics are extremely complex, physics is extremely difficult to get your mind around. But the Gospels aren't complex theoretical reflections on mysterious truths — and they can't be understood as such. They are four descriptions of how Jesus struggled to share his love of God with others, and how his struggle succeeded. The Gospel writers relate this success to us as simple Good News that Jesus invited others to enjoy and spread.

With the help of my retreat director, I stopped looking for hidden lessons in the Gospel narratives. When I began to reread the Gospels without the prejudice of my assumptions, it became clear that, despite many differences in the four texts, each evangelist's narrative zeroed in on the same thing: Jesus' passionate drive to teach by his words and his actions. Biblical scholars have pointed out that we don't know precisely how the Gospel texts reached the form in which they are now presented in the Bible. The Gospel of Luke glances at this fact when it begins with the note that accounts (yes, he says "accounts") had been handed down to the evangelist's generation by those who had witnessed Jesus' ministry [Lk.1:2]. Then the evangelist promises to organize this material so that the reader might come to "realize the certainty of the teachings" [Lk.1:4]. All the Gospel authors (or, if you like, all the editors and copyists who arranged the work of the original authors into the various manuscripts from which our modern Bibles are translated) seem to share this purpose: to make it plain that Jesus taught about God's determination to bring his work of creation to glorious fulfillment in us, his children.

Years ago on retreat, when my director nudged me to take a careful look at precisely what the Gospels say, I began to see them as attempts to let readers hear what Jesus struggled to teach his first disciples to hear: good news. With my director's encouragement to note the simple facts and details set down by the evangelists, I began to feel that even someone as benighted as myself could begin to take in the Gospel's simple message.

WHY A SIMPLE GUIDE TO THE GOSPELS MIGHT HELP YOU

When I look back on my difficulty in noticing Jesus' simple proclamation of the Good News, I take comfort in the fact that my denseness isn't unique. For example, when Mark describes Jesus visiting Nazareth, his old neighbors are said to be so astonished by his teaching that they couldn't believe it. They ask, "Where did this man get all this?" [Mk.6:2]. What they heard seemed too good to be true, so they resolved the tension they felt between surprise and suspicion by choosing to be annoyed: "They took offense at him" [Mk.6:3]. Mark and the other evangelists relate such moments of rejection as dead ends—moments when the story they're telling comes to a temporary halt. In other scenes, however, doubt and astonishment don't end with a rejection of the Good News but lead to an awareness of its power to move the heart. For example, Luke describes the disciples' first response to seeing Jesus after his resurrection as a mix of bafflement and glee: "They were still incredulous for joy and were amazed" [Lk.24:41]. Here, the disciples' delight is said to be as real as their disbelief. A sense of befuddlement ("How can this be?") grips them even as they're filled with joy. One feeling doesn't cancel the other. Luke is telling us that doubts and suspicions needn't overwhelm us with dismay even when they're striking us with full force. What good news!

If you, like me (and like many disciples before us), have been confused by parts of the Gospel narratives, you too might benefit from some simple comments about each scene and event—such as my director's comment about the people who found Jesus fascinating. And you, like me, might be helped by noting that all of Jesus' followers had to grapple with his simple message before they could accept it. For instance, when the Gospel of Mark describes events after the resurrection, it portrays Jesus taking many disciples to task for their stubbornness: "He appeared to them and rebuked them for their unbelief and hardness of heart because they had not believed those who saw him after he had been raised" [Mk.16:14]. Recall, however, what Jesus says next to these slow learners: "He said to them, 'Go into the whole world and proclaim the Gospel to every creature'" [Mk.16:15]. Here Jesus entrusts the announcement of the Gospel—the Good News—to the very individuals who, when they first heard reports of the resurrection, couldn't believe them. It's natural to assume that, as these first disciples headed off to fulfill their commission to proclaim the Good News, they needed to review with one another what they thought the Good News was. They would have asked one another such questions as, "What was it he said that time we were caught in the storm; and what did we say in response?" As they recalled their various experiences of what Jesus had said and done, they would have helped one another review the recent past until they began to see a clear and communicable message—a message that others could grasp as Good News. In turn, those who heard this message began to write accounts of what they heard so still others could hear about Jesus and his struggle to proclaim God's truth as Good News. Each Gospel proclaims this Good News, but each one proclaims it in a slightly different way.

SOME DIFFERENCES IN LUKE'S GOSPEL ACCOUNT

History: The Gospel according to Luke is the first volume of a two-volume work. In his second volume, the Acts of the Apostles, the author (whom we call Luke, though we can't be certain of his identity) describes what Jesus' followers did with the Good News after Jesus' resurrection and ascension. Luke's explicit intention was to write a reliable history of what Jesus taught and how his teaching spread. We know this because he states his purpose at the opening of his first volume by addressing someone called Theophilus and assuring him he's got his facts right: "I'm writing a methodical report of events, Theophilus, so you can be confident in the things you've been taught."

Salvation: like Mark, Luke tells stories. But, unlike Mark, he doesn't urge the reader forward at a breathtaking pace. Luke carefully sets down scenes and events that reveal an underlying truth about the actions of the God who promised to keep his people safe (recall the First Commandment as it's set down at the beginning of Chapter 20 in Exodus: "I, the Lord, am your God—*who brought you out of the land of Egypt, that place of slavery.* Have no other gods!" [emphasis added]). Luke wants Theophilus (and anyone else who reads his account) to see the full sweep of the story of how God, through Jesus, was faithful to the promises he made to his children—the people of Israel—and how the Good News invites all people to see themselves as children of God. In his Gospel, Luke doesn't tell this history by listing precise places, dates, and circumstances. He presents a series of vignettes that reveal a simple, clear story: first, Jesus taught that the God who made a Covenant with Israel was trustworthy; second, Jesus' suffering, death, and resurrection revealed that God's promises were indeed trustworthy; third, the Good News embodied in Jesus' teaching and actions was to be shared with everyone.

Inclusivity: the New Testament epistle writer Paul may have the title Apostle to the Gentiles. But the Gospel of Luke tells the story of Jesus in a way that also makes it plain that his Good News was for anyone willing to hear it. "Here," says Luke, "let me give you some examples of how that was so."

For other matters stressed in Luke's Gospel, see the index.

A TRANSLATION CHALLENGE

The Gospels were written in Greek. Many Gospel translations, including those in lectionaries used for formal church services, have been prepared by commissions of scholars. These translations not only render into English the words of the Greek text but also retain the original rhetorical phrasings. Because ancient Greek phrasing is different from modern English expression, a strictly literal translation is often hard to follow. The simplicity of an evangelist's message can escape us when a translation retains its original (and unfamiliar) turns of phrase.

When preachers begin a homily, they often rephrase whatever text has just been proclaimed. They want to make sure we know what the text actually says before they begin to comment on it. So, after a reading, they're likely to say something like, "Did you notice what the evangelist was saying there? Let me put it another way, just so we don't miss his point." Like a preacher's careful rephrasing of a text, my translation of Luke's Gospel in this simple guide spells out anything that might be muddled or missed in a strictly literal translation of the original Greek words and phrases. The translation also includes occasional explanatory remarks that, in other translations, are relegated to footnotes or the accompanying commentary. I've put such explanations within the passages to let you keep reading Luke's Good News without having to stop to look up unfamiliar references.

ACKNOWLEDGMENTS

My comments after each section of my translation are derived from the study of many scripture commentaries. I am indebted in particular to the richness of the notes and commentary by Luke Timothy Johnson, published in the Sacra Pagina series of studies of the New Testament, and to the wealth of information in the notes and commentary of Joseph A. Fitzmyer, SJ, published as part of the Anchor Bible.

Many people encouraged me during the writing of the manuscript and helped me with comments on it. Thank you to Bridget Leonard, who worked long and hard as a literary agent for this work, and to Carole Sargent for her guidance at Georgetown University's Office of Scholarly and Literary Publication. And thank you to the parishioners at the parishes where I worked—especially to Dorothy Davis, Agnes Williams, Jayne Ikard, and Tom and Mary

Biddle. Other helpful comments came from my sister, Morgan, and from my friends Jean Reynolds and Alan Wynroth. I am grateful to my provincial superior of the Maryland Province of the Jesuits, who allowed me the time to write this book, and to all my supportive Jesuit brothers—especially James P. M. Walsh, SJ.

ONE

Preparation for the Birth of Jesus

PROLOGUE [LK.1:1–4]

¹ Many have set down a narrative of all the matters that came to pass in our midst—² trying to set them down just as they were reported to us by those who were eyewitnesses and ministers of the word from the beginning. ³ So it seemed good to me, after careful study of those matters from their beginnings, that I should also write them down in an orderly fashion for you, noble Theophilus, ⁴ so you may see the truth of the instruction you've received.

———≈≈≈———

Before Luke begins to present a narrative, he offers an assurance that it's accurate. He describes himself as someone who's pulled a number of reports into a structured and reliable account of a story for someone called Theophilus—who, judging by his Greek name, was a non-Jewish student, acquaintance, or friend of the author. It's as if Theophilus had said to the writer of this account, "Look, during my instruction, I heard several versions of events. How am I to put them all together?"

The casual reader of this opening statement, or prologue, might wonder what matters, eyewitnesses, and instruction are being referred to. But anyone who knows a little about the Gospels knows

1

they describe what Jesus said as he proclaimed the coming of God's kingdom. So, as Luke begins his Gospel, we know he's promising to set down a description of Jesus' work [v.1]. He'll be putting in readable order information passed down by those who first heard, and then spread Jesus' teaching [v.2]. Luke hopes his careful presentation of these various accounts [v.3] will help Theophilus clarify and strengthen his grasp of Jesus' message [v.4].

HOW THE BIRTH OF JOHN WAS ANNOUNCED [LK.1:5–17]

⁵ In the days of King Herod of Judea, there was a priest named Zechariah who served in the cohort of Abijah, one of the priestly divisions that rotated service in the Temple. His wife was of the daughters of Aaron. Her name was Elizabeth. ⁶ They were both righteous with God, walking blamelessly in the way of the Lord's commands. ⁷ But they had no child because Elizabeth was barren. And both were advanced in years. ⁸ It happened that he was serving his priestly turn before God. ⁹ He'd been chosen by his division by lot to enter the Lord's sanctuary to burn incense. ¹⁰ At the time of incense, a multitude prayed outside the sanctuary. ¹¹ An angel of the Lord appeared to him and stood at the right of the altar of incense. ¹² Zechariah was startled by what he saw, and fear seized him. ¹³ But the angel told him, "Don't be afraid, Zechariah; your prayer was heard. Your wife Elizabeth will bear a son, and you will name him John. ¹⁴ He'll be your joy and delight, and many will rejoice at his birth. ¹⁵ He'll be great before the Lord. Drinking neither wine nor strong brew, he'll be filled with the Holy Spirit even in his mother's womb. ¹⁶ Because of him, many children of Israel will turn back to the Lord, their God. ¹⁷ He'll go before the Lord with the spirit of Elijah to turn the hearts of parents to their children, and the disobedient to the wisdom of what's right. He'll prepare the people to be ready for the Lord."

—————〰〰〰—————

Luke begins his story by describing Zechariah, a low-ranking priest, carrying out a ritual in the Jerusalem Temple—a ritual for which his group of priests was responsible at scheduled intervals [vv.5a, 8–9]. We also hear that Zechariah's wife descended from the priestly tribe of Aaron [v.5b]. Though both of them took the Covenant seriously (see Dt.5:1–2) by following its commands [v.6], they had never been blessed with a child, and they were now growing old [v.7].

Luke interrupts the ritual of raising incense and prayers to God [v.10] with the extraordinary appearance of a messenger from God—an appearance for which Zechariah wasn't prepared [vv.11–12]. We may find it easy to suppose that neither was he ready to heed the angel's advice to abandon fear—nor to credit the news that Elizabeth was pregnant, nor to accept that the child's name was divinely chosen [v.13]. Ready or not, says Luke, Zechariah heard more astonishing information: rejoicing over this child would spread far outside the family [v.14]. From the very beginning of his life, the child would be dedicated to God, whose Spirit would fill him, freeing him from the need for any other stimulant [v.15]. The child would grow up to help the children of God—the Israelites—repent [v.16]. In fact, according to Luke's description of the angel's promises, Zechariah's boy would have the same sort of power Elijah had (see Sir.48:10)—the power to turn hearts away from selfishness and incline them to God [v.17].

HOW ZECHARIAH AND ELIZABETH REACTED TO THE ANNOUNCEMENT [LK.1:18–25]

[18] *Zechariah asked the angel, "How will I know this? I'm old, and my wife's advanced in years." [19] The angel said, "I am Gabriel; I stand before God, and was sent to tell you this. [20] Look: you'll be mute, unable to speak until these things happen, because you didn't accept my words, which will be fulfilled in their time." [21] Now, the people waiting outside the sanctuary were puzzled by Zechariah's delay. [22] When he came out unable to speak, they knew he'd had a vision in the sanctuary. Despite all his gestures, he said nothing. [23] When his days of service at the Jerusalem Temple were completed, he went to his home in the hills. [24] After that time, his wife Elizabeth became pregnant but hid herself for five months. [25] She said, "Now, at this time, the Lord has acted on my behalf to take away my disgrace before others."*

———◦◦◦———

As Luke tells it, Zechariah wanted more than the angel's word to help him see past what seemed to him an insurmountable obstacle: old age [v.18]. Though Zechariah's incredulity, like Abraham's (see Gn.15:1–8), was quite natural, the angel challenged it. The lesson the angel wanted Zechariah to learn was simple: God's word should be believed [v.19]. Zechariah was then given the gift of silence: he could reflect quietly on Gabriel's lesson. We hear that Gabriel also nudged him to be patient, reminding him it takes time to fulfill God's word [v.20].

Speaking of patience, Luke says that those who were offering their prayers while Zechariah offered incense became anxious at his delayed reappearance [v.21]. Although Luke tells us the people were sure Zechariah had had a vision, he also says Zechariah's frantic miming didn't help him express what he saw [v.22]. He goes back to his village somewhere in the Judean hill country, still unable to communicate his vision [v.23].

After Luke reports that Elizabeth became pregnant, he doesn't explain why she retired from sight [v.24]. But he does say Elizabeth gave thanks to God for acting on her behalf and blessing her despite the fact that others had thought she'd been shamed [v.25]. Apparently feeling no need to gloat or flaunt her long-delayed luck, she kept to herself, savoring her blessing and giving thanks for it.

MARY IS ASKED TO BE THE MOTHER OF JESUS [LK.1:26–38]

²⁶ When Elizabeth was in her sixth month, the angel Gabriel was sent by God to a town in Galilee called Nazareth. ²⁷ He was sent to a virgin engaged to a man named Joseph, of the line of David. The virgin's name was Mary. ²⁸ He went up to her and said, "Hail, most favored. The Lord is with you." ²⁹ But this message bewildered her, and she wondered what it might mean. ³⁰ The angel said, "Do not be afraid, Mary. You have found favor with God. ³¹ Look now: you will conceive in your womb, and bring forth a son, and call his name Jesus. ³² He will be great. He will be called Son of the Most High. The Lord God will give him the throne of his father, David. ³³ He will reign over the house of Jacob forever. His kingdom will have no end." ³⁴ Mary said, "How can this be? I'm not yet with my husband." [35] *The angel said, "The Holy Spirit will come upon you. The power of the Most High will overshadow you. Therefore, the one born will be holy—will be called Son of God.* [36] *Imagine: your cousin, Elizabeth, has conceived a son in her old age. She is in her sixth month—she, who was called barren.* [37] *With God, nothing will be impossible."* [38] *Mary said, "I am the Lord's handmaid. Let it be as you say." The angel left her.*

—————∞∞∞—————

Because Luke told us Elizabeth and Zechariah both descended from priestly clans (see 1:5), they may seem likely agents for God's work. But Luke tells us nothing about Mary other than her town and marital status. Her betrothed, not she, is descended from David [vv.26–27]. We know no reason why God should single her out. She herself is baffled by the angel's presence and greeting [vv.28–29]. Like Zechariah (see 1:13), Mary is told not to fear [v.30a]. Then the angel repeats the information that God is deeply pleased to act in her [v.30b], and proceeds to explain the effects of that action: a child will be born and is to be named Jesus [v.31]; Jesus will receive greatness directly from God, his Father, and will also be given the kingdom of his ancestor, David [v.32]; and his rule over that kingdom will never end [v.33].

According to Luke, Mary asked only about the first of these extraordinary promises—that is, how she could bear a child if she hadn't yet been with a man [v.34]. Luke describes the angel asking Mary to consider: "How has any part of God's plan come to pass? Through God's doing, of course!" [v.35]. Then, with the news about Elizabeth's condition, the angel offers an example of God's way of working [v.36]. That's followed by a gentle nudge to remember what the Creator can do [v.37]. Finally, Luke describes Mary remembering: "How could I forget! I am God's own work. So, let his work continue in me, just as you've described it" [v.38].

MARY VISITS ELIZABETH [LK.1:39–56]

[39] Mary traveled speedily to Zechariah's town in the Judean hill country. [40] She entered Zechariah's house and greeted Elizabeth. [41] When Elizabeth heard Mary's greeting, the babe in her womb leapt. Elizabeth was filled with the Holy Spirit. [42] She cried, "You're blessed among women. Blessed is the fruit of your womb. [43] How is it that the mother of my Lord comes to me? [44] When your greeting struck my ears, the babe in my womb leapt with joy. [45] Blessed is the one who believed that what the Lord spoke would happen." [46] Mary said, "My soul exalts the Lord. [47] My spirit delights in God, my Savior. [48] He looked on his servant's lowliness. Now all generations will call me blessed. [49] He who is mighty has done great things to me. His name is holy. [50] His mercy is for those who fear him, generation after generation. [51] His arm did mighty deeds. He routed the proud of heart. [52] He brought the mighty down from their thrones. He lifted up the lowly. [53] He filled the hungry with good things. He sent the rich away empty. [54] He helped Israel, his servant, to remember his mercy. [55] This was just as he promised our fathers, Abraham and his descendants, forever." [56] Mary stayed with Elizabeth about three months. Then she returned home.

———❦———

Luke describes Mary as eager to be with Elizabeth in her time of good fortune [vv.39–40]. At the merest greeting from Mary, Elizabeth is filled with a sense of God's presence and feels a leaping in her womb [v.41]. The divine Spirit overwhelms her with an awareness of the favor God has shown Mary [v.42]. She can't believe Mary's impulse was to share her blessings with her [v.43]. After she describes her experience of the Spirit, she identifies what it is that makes Mary blessed: her belief in the word of the Lord [vv.44–45].

Mary's grateful celebration of belief, as Luke describes it, might be expected from any young Jew who believes the word of God. Psalms and other parts of scripture that we now call the Old Testament told her to expect ultimate delight only from God [v.46]: only God can make us rejoice [v.47]; lowliness is no obstacle to God's blessings [v.48]; we can expect God to do mighty deeds [v.49]; those who trust in God's patience and kindness are never disappointed [v.50]; those who are arrogant are ultimately undone [v.51]; the haughty, who think they need no help, get none, while the humble get aid [v.52]; indeed, the humble are drenched with blessings, while those who need no help remain helpless [v.53]. According to Luke, Mary proclaimed that God's basic command to Abraham and all Israel was to trust in divine love and mercy [v.54–55]. Like Abraham, Mary was willing to be utterly dependent on God. Luke says she enjoyed a long visit with her fellow believer [v.56].

REACTION TO THE BIRTH OF ELIZABETH'S CHILD
[LK.1:57–66]

[57] *The time came for Elizabeth to deliver her child, and she gave birth to a son.* [58] *Her neighbors and relatives heard the Lord had been gracious to her, and they rejoiced with her.* [59] *These friends and relatives gathered on the eighth day for the boy's circumcision, calling him "Zechariah," after his father.* [60] *But his mother said, "No, he'll be called John."* [61] *"Not one of your relatives is called by that name," they said.* [62] *They gestured to Zechariah [treating him as though he was deaf as well as mute] to ask what he wanted him called.* [63] *He asked for a tablet and surprised them by writing, "John is his name."* [64] *Straightway his mouth opened and his tongue spoke, blessing God.* [65] *The neighbors were awestruck. Everywhere in the Judean hill country these matters were bruited about.* [66] *All who heard about these things took them to heart and wondered, "What will this child be?" Indeed, the hand of the Lord was with him.*

———————

Luke tells us that, by the time of Elizabeth's delivery, family and neighbors knew the Lord had blessed her, and they were eager to celebrate the birth of a boy to carry on Zechariah's name [vv.57–59]. But their expectations were upset by several surprises that highlighted the extraordinary nature of this child's birth. It seems Zechariah had communicated to Elizabeth the angel's instructions about naming the child (see 1:13)—a name Elizabeth obviously accepted [v.60]. We hear that, when her relatives objected [v.61] and assumed her husband would overrule her [v.62], they were corrected [v.63].

This correction, followed so suddenly by Zechariah's voluble thanksgiving [v.64], left them flabbergasted—but not so astonished that they didn't spread the story everywhere [v.65]. According to Luke, people who heard the story kept thinking about it, asking themselves what further marvels might attend this child. Then he reminds us the child was special because of the way in which God was at work in him [v.66].

The opening moments of this episode are described by Luke as a typical celebration of the Covenant with God: rejoicing at the news of a birth; taking delight that God has (finally) blessed Elizabeth; gathering to witness a circumcision, marking a child with the same sign that marked Abraham as a child of God; expecting a son to bear his father's name and, perhaps, carry on his priestly work; and disapproving of a name that didn't follow tradition. Then Luke alters this picture of domestic and community joy by depicting the unexpected—that is, by depicting God at work. But if the people in the story had truly trusted that they were constantly in God's care, why would they be surprised by signs of that care?

WHAT ZECHARIAH SAID IN HIS BLESSING OF GOD
[LK.1:67–80]

[67] Zechariah was filled with the Holy Spirit and spoke as a prophet of God's truth. [68] "Blessed be the Lord God of Israel. He has come to his People and redeemed them. [69] From the house of David, his servant, he raised up a horn to save us. [70] He spoke this promise through the mouths of the holy ones of old, the prophets: [71] 'He saved us from our enemies, from the hand of all who hate us' [Ps.106:10]. [72] He was merciful to our fathers. He was mindful always of the Covenant. [73] He remembered the oath he swore to Abraham, our father, to give us a gift. [74] That gift was freedom from enemies so we might worship him without fear. [75] Yes, that we might worship him holily and rightly all our days. [76] You, my child, will be called a prophet of the Most High. You will go before the Lord to prepare his way. [77] You will make salvation known to his people in forgiveness of their sins. [78] Yes, you'll make known God's tender mercy, bursting on us from on high. [79] Indeed, it will dawn on those in darkness, in death's

shadow, and guide us in the path of peace." [80] *The child grew and became strong in spirit. He tarried in the wilderness until the day he was made known to Israel.*

———⟨𝕰/𝕰/𝕰⟩———

Here, Luke relates the blessing Zechariah spoke with a flood of praise when his tongue was freed (see 1:64), telling us, first, that his prophecy—his proclamation of God's truth—was inspired by the Spirit [v.67]. Like Mary's expression of praise (see 1:46–55), Zechariah's cries of glory, thanks, and trust echoed the words of scripture. We hear him blessing God as the Psalms had taught him to do, praising him for his care; proclaiming his belief that someone will free them from sin [v.68]—a redeemer who will be as strong and confident as a horned animal, and who will face down danger and peril as no one from the house of David has done before [v.69]. Luke says Zechariah also said God's powerful protection of his children had been proclaimed over and over again [v.70]—especially in the Psalms [v.71]—and though his children forgot the Covenant, God did not [v.72]. Instead, God kept recalling what he first promised Abraham [v.73]: he would constantly help his children remain faithful to him [vv.74–75].

Then we hear how Zechariah imagined God working through his son [v.76]: his child would tell people about freedom from sinful ways [v.77] and about God's deep desire to be merciful and forgiving [v.78]. Not even the darkness of death can dim the bright promise of God's graciousness, says Zechariah. Rather, God can lead those caught up in deadly selfishness onto a path of peace [v.79]. Luke suggests John grew up preparing only to proclaim God's mercy [v.80].

TWO
Jesus Is Born, Named, and Instructed

JESUS IS BORN, AND HIS BIRTH IS ANNOUNCED [LK.2:1–14]

¹ Caesar Augustus decreed a census of the whole world. ² Part of the census was when Quirinius was governor of Syria. ³ All traveled to their family town to register. ⁴ Joseph went from the city of Nazareth in Galilee to Judea, to the city of David, Bethlehem, because Joseph descended from the house and line of David. ⁵ He traveled with Mary, his betrothed who was with child. ⁶ Now, while they were there, the time came for her to give birth. ⁷ She bore her firstborn son, swaddled him with cloth, and laid him in a manger. There wasn't space for them in the crowded upper room where caravan groups lodged. ⁸ Shepherds were nearby, watching at night in the fields over their flocks. ⁹ An angel of the Lord stood there. The Lord's glory surrounded them. And their fright completely overwhelmed them. ¹⁰ "Don't be afraid," the angel said. "Look now; I bring good news so all may rejoice. ¹¹ This day, a savior is born to you in the city of David. He is God's Anointed One, the Lord. ¹² Seek this sign: a swaddled infant lying in a manger." ¹³ All at once, a multitude of the heavenly host was there with the angel, praising God. ¹⁴ They said, "Glory in the highest to God. On earth, peace to those pleasing to God."

Luke promised to relate certain events to Theophilus (see 1:1–3), and here he describes how the emperor of the "whole world"—that is, the Roman Empire—commanded a census of the Roman provinces [vv.1–2]. This required Joseph to travel to Bethlehem to register [vv.3–4]—a requirement that couldn't be put off for personal reasons [v.5]. While Joseph and Mary were caught in the bustle of imperial business, Mary also managed maternal concerns—away from the crush of a packed hostelry [vv.6–7]. While people throughout the empire were busily accomplishing an elaborate civic task, God was quietly doing his work through one woman.

According to Luke, this divine work wasn't revealed to the hordes obeying the emperor's decree. Instead, it was told to a few shepherds tending to ordinary business [v.8]. The general population was caught up in important official business; in contrast, Luke describes shepherds going about their simple daily chores—where they suddenly find themselves confronted by God's messenger and enveloped in God's astonishing light [v.9]. Without much explanation, the angel gives these stunned people a task: seek God's anointed one and find him in an infant lodged in a temporary home [vv.10–12]. Luke says the angel, joined by other heavenly creatures, sang out a song of rejoicing [vv.13–14]—in which the shepherds may have joined as they accepted the task given them by the angel.

THE ANNOUNCEMENT OF JESUS' BIRTH CAUSES WONDER— HE'S NAMED [LK.2:15–21]

15 When the angels disappeared, the shepherds said, "Let's go to Bethlehem. Let's see what wonder's been done—what it is the Lord's revealed to us." 16 They hurried off, and found Mary, Joseph, and the baby in the manger. 17 At the sight, they reported what they'd been told about the child. 18 [Later,] all who heard the shepherds' story were amazed at what they heard. 19 Mary meanwhile kept all this in her heart and turned it over and over there. 20 The shepherds went back to their work glorifying and praising God for all they heard and all they saw. It was just as they'd been told. 21 When eight days brought the time for circumci-

sion, he was called Jesus—the name the angel called him before he was conceived.

———⸙⸙⸙———

Luke says the shepherds responded to the angel's commission and their heavenly burst of rejoicing (see 2:14) by setting off to confirm the good news they'd heard [v.15]. We hear their quest was quickly accomplished [v.16] and that they poured out their story to Mary and Joseph [v.17]—perhaps even repeating to them the heavenly song of praise. When others heard about the shepherds' experience, they were as surprised as the shepherds had been at first [v.18]. One can wonder what people made of this story when their amazement wore off. Was it like Mary's reaction? Luke tells us that her reaction to the shepherds' joyful proclamation of her son's identity was to contemplate their message over and over again [v.19]. Was it like the shepherds' reaction? Luke says they too turned over and over their experience of God's presence and words by speaking of that experience [v.20]. According to Luke, the shepherds were the first to announce to people at large the good news about the Messiah—that is, "the Christ," "the Anointed One" of God (see 2:11). This Messiah was the same "Lord" who, as Mary was told, would bring about an eternal kingdom (see 1:33).

We then read that Jesus, like John, was marked by circumcision as a child of God (see 1:59)—just as Abraham was first marked. In this way, Mary and Joseph proclaimed that Jesus, like them, would embrace God's Covenant and commands. They themselves followed God's command by naming the child Jesus—that is, "Help, Lord Yahweh!" (see 1:31)—as the angel had told Mary to do [v.21]. Here, Luke depicts a Jewish man and woman intent on following the Law that was set down to help the children of God remember the Covenant—their Covenant with the God who had promised to care for them, and to whom they could cry, "Help, Lord Yahweh!"

PRESENTING THE CHILD JESUS [LK.2:22–38]

[22] When the day came for the purification ceremony required by the Law of Moses, they brought the child to Jerusalem to present him to the Lord. [23] This followed the Law of the Lord: "Every male that opens the womb will be consecrated to the Lord" [Ex.13:2]. [24] They also offered sacrifice in accord with the Law: "two little doves" [Lv.12:8]. [25] Now, in Jerusalem there was a devout, righteous man named Simeon. Filled with the Holy Spirit, he awaited the promised consolation of Israel [see, e.g., Is.61:2]. [26] It had been revealed to him by the Holy Spirit that he would not see death until he saw the Messiah of the Lord. [27] He was led by the Spirit to the Temple when Jesus' parents brought him there to do what was customary according to the Law. [28] Simeon took him into his arms, blessed God, and said: [29] "Now you can let your servant go in peace, according to your word. [30] For my eyes have seen your salvation—[31] a salvation prepared before all people. [32] Yes, light enlightening the Gentiles; glory for your people Israel." [33] His mother and father were surprised that this was said of him. [34] Simeon blessed them, and to Mary he said, "Behold, this one is set for the collapse and ascent of many in Israel—a sign that will be opposed. [35] A sword will pierce even you. Yes, the brooding of many hearts will be laid open." [36] Anna was also there—a prophetess, the daughter of Phanuel of Asher's tribe. She was of great age. She had lived with her husband for seven years. [37] Then she was a widow for eighty-four years. She never left the Temple. She fasted and prayed night and day. [38] She thanked God she was there at that moment. Then she spoke about the child to all who awaited the redemption of Jerusalem.

—————

Luke described Mary and Joseph celebrating Jesus' birth as God's gift (see 2:21). Here, he says they gave witness that their child's life belonged to God [v.22] by celebrating rituals set down in scripture—rituals that stress God's governance of life [vv.23–24]. Luke then describes two other people who gave witness to their belief that God can purify and redirect our longings.

He says Simeon went up to the Temple believing in God's promise of salvation, the promise to send someone specifically chosen or anointed—the "Messiah"—to bring people from misery to consolation [vv.25–27]. Simeon gave thanks [v.28], saying he saw God's plan of salvation in the child [vv.29–30] — a plan that would save all people [vv.31–32]. According to Luke, this profession of belief in God's plan startled the parents [v.33] — an amazement to which Simeon added, perhaps, when he warned them that God's work through this child would disturb many [v.34] — even Mary would be troubled [v.35a]. Simeon concludes his witness with a simple description of how God works in all of us: by showing us what's in our hearts [v.35b]. The implication seems to be that people will discover what their hearts truly long for when they see God's plan unfold in the life of this child — a life that will delight or upset their deepest desires. Then Luke immediately introduces someone who is moved with delight. He says Anna, a woman of ancient Jewish lineage who continually thanked God for his goodness [vv.36–37], spoke of the child to anyone willing to share her hopes [v.38].

JESUS GROWS UP IN GOD'S CARE [LK.2:39–52]

39 After Jesus' parents had done everything according to the Law of the Lord at the purification ceremony [see 2:22], they returned to Nazareth, their town in Galilee. 40 The child grew and became strong, filled with wisdom and God's gracious favor. 41 And each year, his parents went up to Jerusalem for the Passover Feast. 42 When he reached twelve, following their custom, they went to the Feast. 43 After the Feast, they headed home. Young Jesus stayed in Jerusalem, but his parents didn't know this. 44 They thought he was with the caravan as they traveled for a day, at which point, they sought him among their friends and family. 45 When they didn't find him, they went back to Jerusalem to look for him. 46 They found him three days later. He was sitting with teachers in the Temple, listening and questioning. 47 All who heard him were surprised by his quickness and responses. 48 When his parents saw him, they were taken aback. His mother said, "Son, why have you done this to us? Your father and I have been searching frantically for you." 49 He said, "Why did you have to search? Didn't you know I'd be in my Father's house?" 50 They didn't understand his words to them. 51 So, he went down from the mount of Jerusalem to Nazareth obediently. And his mother pondered all this in her heart. ⁵² *Jesus grew up in wisdom—and in height—and in the favor of God and man.*

———◌◌◌———

Just above, Luke said Simeon and Anna claimed Jesus would play an extraordinary role in God's plan of salvation. But here Luke describes the ordinary life of a Jewish family. Even the assertion that Jesus grew in wisdom and divine favor might be made about any child who was being taught by his parents to take the Covenant seriously [vv.39–41].

True, the confusion Luke describes during the family's return from celebrating a Passover feast in Jerusalem is remarkable, but it could arise in any group of travelers [vv.42–45]. And yes, the resolution of the mix-up is striking, but it's not unheard-of for a twelve-year-old to lose all track of time pursuing a special interest—in this case, sinking so deeply into a discussion about God that even learned adults were fully engaged [vv.46–47]. We hear the voice of all anxious parents in Mary's question: "Why didn't you let us know where you were?" [v.48]. Jesus' answer is similar to what every preoccupied adolescent says in such situations: "I thought you knew." Luke describes both the parents and the child as puzzled, each wondering how the other could be so oblivious to the obvious [vv.49–50]. Luke then tells us that Jesus realized he had to practice obedience—that is, that he had more to learn. Mary too, he says, savored her experiences—that is, she had more to learn [v.51]. Then he tells us what happened when Jesus continued to learn: he grew in wisdom to the delight of both God and others [v.52].

THREE

John, Preaching Righteousness, Baptizes Jesus—Which Is Pleasing to God

JOHN PREACHES REPENTANCE [LK.3:1–9]

1 In the fifteenth year of the reign of Tiberius Caesar (when Pontius Pilate was governor of Judea, and Herod was tetrarch of Galilee; and Philip, his brother, tetrarch of the Ituraea-Trachonitis region; and Lysanias tetrarch of Abilene; 2 and during the high priesthood of Annas and Caiaphas), the word of God came to John, son of Zechariah, in the wilderness. 3 John then went through the Jordan valley preaching a baptism of repentance for forgiveness of sins. 4 As is written in the book of the prophet Isaiah, his was "a voice calling in the desert: 'Prepare the way of the Lord; make his paths straight. 5 Every valley shall be filled, every mountain and hill shall be leveled. Crooked ways will be straightened, and rough ways smoothed. 6 All flesh shall see the salvation of God'" [Is.40:3–5]. 7 To the crowds who came seeking baptism, John said, "Spawn of vipers! Who warned you the wrath is coming? 8 Do what springs from repentance. Don't start telling yourselves, 'We have Abraham as a father!' Listen, God can raise children of Abraham from these stones! 9 Right now the ax is aimed at the trees' roots. Every unproductive tree will be cut down and thrown in the fire."

—⟋⟍⟋⟍—

Luke moves forward in time with a long and formal note about the year. He says that, while the world was busy about its business (see 2:1–3), God was also working out the divine plan—even in the wilderness [vv.1–2]. He describes John responding promptly and without any question to what he felt was God's command to proclaim repentance by offering a public washing (baptism) to let people give witness that they needed cleansing, renewal, and forgiveness from God for turning away from him [v.3]. Luke says that John's preaching repeated the words of others who had spoken out (prophesied) about the need to seek forgiveness and to ask for a renewal of the Covenant. In particular, he was echoing the words written in the Book of Isaiah: "If you're seeking a way back to the Lord, your God, don't plan a convoluted trip; go directly to him [v.4]. If you do that, you'll find the way made easy by the Lord [v.5]. In fact, you'll find God *bringing* forgiveness to you—yes, to you, and all around you [v.6]."

According to Luke, John said those who approached God proudly (see v.8) were deadly snakes whose poisonous effects God wouldn't tolerate [v.7]. God raised up Abraham. And it's God, says John, who raises up Abraham's children. So, turn away from pride in yourself [v.8]. Repentance and self-righteousness are as plainly different as fresh fruit and rotten apples [v.9].

JOHN REVIEWS THE COMMANDMENTS, GIVES GOOD NEWS, AND BAPTIZES JESUS [LK.3:10–22]

[10] The crowds, warned by John against pride [see 3:8], asked what they should do. [11] He said, "If you have two shirts, give to someone with none; the same with food." [12] Tariff collectors too sought baptism. They asked, "Teacher, what should we do?" [13] "Collect no more than you're supposed to," he said. [14] Even soldiers asked, "What should we do?" He said, "Don't extort money by intimidating others. Be satisfied with what you're paid." [15] People were agog. They asked themselves whether John might be God's Anointed One. [16] "I baptize you with water," he said. "Someone stronger than I is coming, whose sandal I'm not fit to fasten. He'll baptize you with the Holy Spirit and fire. [17] His flail is in his hand.

He's at work on the threshing floor. He'll gather the wheat into his barn. The chaff he'll burn with a fire too hot to put out." [18] *He used many other admonishments to preach this good news.* [19] *(John also admonished Herod the tetrarch for marrying his brother's wife, and for other wicked ways.* [20] *Herod added to his wickedness by eventually putting John in prison.)* [21] *Now, after a procession of many who were baptized, Jesus was baptized. He prayed and, as he did so, the heavens opened.* [22] *The Holy Spirit seemed to fall upon him—like the swoop of a dove. A voice coming from heaven said, "You are my beloved Son. I am deeply pleased with you."*

———

Luke says some children of Abraham (see 3:8) asked how to put repentance into practice [v.10]. He says John answered them with a call to notice others' needs. This was a call to follow the commandments—to love God (see Ex.20:3) by regarding one's neighbor with the opposite of envy (see Ex.20:17). He says John also told the Jews who collected various Roman fees, or served in Herod's military forces, not to covet their neighbor's goods [vv.11–14]. When Luke says the crowd was so struck by John's teaching that they thought he might be the Messiah, God's Anointed One, it suggests they heard his teaching as something special—despite the fact that it was simply an admonishment to obey the commandments [v.15]. Next, says Luke, John tried to raise the crowd's expectations about what someone specially chosen or "anointed" by God would look like. First, we hear him describe himself as the lowliest servant of this specially chosen or anointed one. Then we hear him say God's Anointed One would transform hearts not with water, but with the Holy Sprit burning deeply into their souls [v.16]. And if the flame of the Spirit was rejected, a different fire awaited [v.17].

Luke tells us these sorts of words [v.18] provoked some opposition. Herod, he says, heard John's call to repentance—and his specific application of the commandment against covetousness (see Lv.20:21)—and silenced him [vv.19–20]. But we hear that Jesus heard the call to turn to God and celebrated it with baptism—an action, Luke says, that provoked an enthusiastic display of the enjoyment God takes in our acceptance of the Covenant [vv.21–22].

WHERE DID JESUS COME FROM? [LK.3:23–38]

23 Jesus was about thirty when he began his ministry as the son—so it was thought—of Joseph, who was son of Heli, 24 son of Matthat, son of Levi, son of Melchi, son of Jannai, son of Joseph, 25 son of Mattathias, son of Amos, son of Nahum, son of Esli, son of Naggai, 26 son of Maath, son of Mattathias, son of Semein, son of Josech, son of Joda, 27 son of Joanan, son of Rhesa, son of Zerubbabel, son of Shealtiel, son of Neri, 28 son of Melchi, son of Addi, son of Cosam, son of Elmadam, son of Er, 29 son of Joshua, son of Eliezer, son of Jorim, son of Matthat, son of Levi, 30 son of Simeon, son of Judah, son of Joseph, son of Jonam, son of Eliakim, 31 son of Melea, son of Menna, son of Mattatha, son of Nathan, son of David, 32 son of Jesse, son of Obed, son of Boaz, son of Sala, son of Nahshon, 33 son of Amminadab, son of Admin, son of Arni, son of Hezron, son of Perez, son of Judah, 34 son of Jacob, son of Isaac, son of Abraham, son of Terah, son of Nahor, 35 son of Serug, son of Reu, son of Peleg, son of Eber, son of Shelah, 36 son of Cainan, son of Arphaxad, son of Shem, son of Noah, son of Lamech, 37son of Methuselah, son of Enoch, son of Jared, son of Mahalaleel, son of Cainan, 38 son of Enos, son of Seth, son of Adam, the son of God.

—————

Luke has already told us Jesus had been called God's Son—first by an angel, and then by God himself (see 1:32; 3:22). In the first instance, Gabriel declared that Jesus was destined to be given divine glory—that he was entitled to everything that came from his Father, just as a legitimate son is entitled to an inheritance. In the second instance, God's voice proclaimed him his Son when Jesus expressed, through baptism, his desire to have divine glory.

Here, Luke suggests that a share in the divine glory is the destiny God has planned for all human beings from the beginning. He gives us a long list of names without a single comment on any individual. He has pointed out, in effect, that Jesus is connected to many people about whom we know little or nothing. But he has also pointed out that Jesus' connection with them was more intimate than blood. After all, as he notes, Jesus wasn't Joseph's blood kin. They're connected because, from Adam, they're all children of the same God—the God who offers a Covenant that was spelled out to Moses: I am your God; you are my people (see, e.g., Ex.6:7).

What Luke suggests through this simple list is that we should not be surprised if the proclamation of the Covenant that bound all these people together is central to Jesus' ministry [v.23].

FOUR

Though Tempted to Seek Power and Glory, Jesus Seeks to Serve

JESUS IS TEMPTED [LK.4:1–13]

[1] Filled with the Holy Spirit [see 3:22], Jesus left the Jordan valley. Led by the Spirit, he went into the wilderness. [2] After forty days, he was tempted by the devil. Having eaten nothing, he was hungry. [3] The devil said, "If you're the Son of God, tell this stone to become bread." [4] "It's written," said Jesus, "'One doesn't live just on bread' [Dt.8:3]." [5] The devil took him high up and, in one moment, showed him all the world's kingdoms. [6] "I'll give you this world's power and glory. They've been given to me. I can give them to whom I like. [7] All this is yours, if you worship me." [8] "It's written," said Jesus, "'You shall worship the Lord, your God. Serve only him' [Dt.6:13]." [9] He took him to Jerusalem, high on the Temple. "If you're the Son of God," he said, "fling yourself down. [10] It's written, 'He will order his angels to protect you' [Ps.91:11]; [11] and, 'Their hands will lift you, keeping you from tripping even on a stone' [Ps.91:12]." [12] "It also says," said Jesus, "'You shall not test the Lord, your God' [Dt.6:16]." [13] The devil tried all sorts of temptations, then left for the time being.

After God proclaimed him his Son (see 3:22), Jesus was inspired by the Spirit, says Luke, to go off by himself—a choice that led to a time of temptation [vv.1–2a]. (This suggests that, if Jesus was filled with the Holy Spirit but was nonetheless tempted, any other child of God will experience temptation.) Luke says Jesus was tempted by the devil to demonstrate the power of his divine sonship by satisfying his hunger miraculously—a temptation he resists by recalling what he'd learned in scripture: because God satisfies our deepest needs, we don't have to fret even about our need to eat [vv.2b–4]. Next, says Luke, the devil appealed to Jesus' ambition, asking him to accept that the world is ruled by wiliness, and that he (the father of lies) is the undisputed lord of all guile. Worship my power, says the devil, and I'll share it with you [vv.5–7]. But Jesus says scripture has taught him that only God is worth worshiping [v.8].

We then hear the devil turn scripture into a tool to help him win his deadly game. Prove the Psalms speak the truth, he says; make God hold you in his hand [vv.9–11]. But Jesus says he's learned from scripture that, if you're going to trust in God's care and goodness, you're not going to challenge him to prove his love [v.12]. Luke's comment that the temptations were over "for a while" alerts us to watch for more in the future [v.13].

JESUS ADDRESSES PEOPLE'S NEED FOR THE GOOD NEWS
[LK.4:14–30]

[14] *Filled with the Spirit [see 3:22], Jesus returned to Galilee. Word about him spread.* [15] *He taught in their synagogues, and everyone praised him.* [16] *He reached Nazareth where he'd been brought up. As usual, he went to the synagogue. There, he stood up to read.* [17] *He was given the scroll of the prophet Isaiah. He unrolled it and found this:* [18] *"The Spirit of the Lord is upon me. He anointed me to preach Good News to the poor. He sent me to bring freedom to captives, to give sight to the blind, to bring relief to the oppressed.* [19] *I am to proclaim a year of forgiveness from the Lord" [Is.61:1–2; 58:6].* [20] *He rolled up the scroll, gave it back to the attendant, and sat down—all eyes on him.* [21] *"Today, this scripture is fulfilled as you listen," he began.* [22] *Everyone commented on his eloquence: "Isn't this Joseph's son?"* [23] *"No doubt," he said, "you'll think of the proverb: 'Physician, heal yourself,' and you'll say, 'Do here at*

home the things we heard you did in Capernaum.' ²⁴ *I say, O, yes indeed, no prophet's welcome in his own country.* ²⁵ *Yes, in Elijah's time, when the sky dried up for three and a half years and famine was in the land, there were many widows in Israel.* ²⁶ *And yet Elijah wasn't sent to one of them, but to a widow in Zarephath in Syria.* ²⁷ *In Elisha's time, lepers in Israel weren't made clean, but Naaman the Syrian was."* ²⁸ *The people in the synagogue were enraged when they heard this.* ²⁹ *They jumped up and rushed him to a cliff where they hoped to throw him off.* ³⁰ *But he slipped away in the midst of it all. And he left.*

Luke says Jesus was admired when he taught as one filled with God's Spirit [vv.14–15]. One might suppose, then, he would also be admired in Nazareth, where he'd grown up [v.16a]. We're told that, when he visited the synagogue there, he was invited to read and comment on scripture [vv.16b–17]. He chose a passage of scripture that pictured God's promise of care and healing being fulfilled [v.18]—a long period, or "year," of gracious forgiveness [v.19]. Luke reports that, when Jesus said now was the time of forgiveness, the crowd was more puzzled by his eloquence than moved by his message [vv.20–22]. He says Jesus guessed they wanted something different. By telling us about Jesus' references to the physician proverb and to "things done" in Capernaum [v.23], Luke suggests Jesus' old neighbors had heard some stories about miracles (not yet described) and that they expected some signs that these stories were true.

Then, says Luke, Jesus challenged their expectations by reminding them how Elijah's and Elisha's calls to trust in God were spurned by the children of God but heeded in foreign lands (see 1 Kgs.17; 2 Kgs.5). Luke tells us that these strong appeals to trust in God's healing power, instead of seeking proof of God's power to heal, provoked a murderous rage in the people of Jesus' hometown [vv.24–29]. He also tells us that Jesus simply walked away from this blind frenzy [v.30].

JESUS CONTINUES TO TEACH — AND HEAL [LK.4:31–44]

[31] Jesus traveled to Capernaum, on the Lake of Galilee, and he taught on the Sabbath. [32] People were surprised he taught with such authority. [33] A man in the synagogue who was bedeviled by an evil spirit began to shout: [34] "Hoo! What's with you and me, Jesus of Nazareth? Come to destroy us? I know who you are, Holy One of God!" [35] "Shush," ordered Jesus. "Out!" The demon shoved the man forward, and left him unharmed. [36] People were amazed: "What's in his words that he can order evil spirits away?" [37] Word about him went around the region. [38] When he left the synagogue, he went to Simon's house where Simon's mother-in-law was suffering from a fever. They spoke to him about her. [39] He stood over her and gave the fever an order. It left. She got up to serve them. [40] At sunset, the sick of all sorts were brought to him. He laid hands on them and healed them. [41] Many who were bedeviled cried out, "You're the Son of God." But he ordered them not to speak because they knew he was the Anointed One. [42] At daybreak, he headed for a secluded spot, but the crowds tried to stop him. [43] "I have to go to other towns to proclaim the Good News of the kingdom of God," he said. "That's why I'm sent." [44] He went to preach in the synagogues all throughout the area.

———※❀❀❀※———

Luke says Jesus went to Capernaum where he'd apparently visited previously (see 4:23), and notes that, on this subsequent visit, Jesus again struck people as a speaker with great power [vv.31–32]—a power they sensed when he banished an unsettling spirit and kept it from spewing its fears about God's might [vv.33–35]. And, he says, people everywhere spoke of Jesus' fearless confidence in facing down evil and revealing its lack of power [vv.36–37].

Then, says Luke, when the people with whom Jesus was staying brought to his attention the need of a woman for relief from a severe fever, Jesus immediately responded to it, and the woman immediately enjoyed the results of the healing [vv.38–39]. He says that Jesus next responded to the needs of many sick people and that, just as he'd silenced the bedeviling spirit in the synagogue (see v.33), he wouldn't let other disturbing spirits define either him or the work he'd been anointed by God to do [vv.40–41]. Luke describes Jesus as also unwilling to let the whole crowd tell him what he should do. Instead, he tells them what he considers his work to be—that is, to tell everyone the Good News that God had sent him to proclaim: God wants everyone to accept the gift of his kingdom [vv.42–43].

Luke has already told us that Jesus' baptism—an action proclaiming his complete acceptance of a loving relationship with God—delighted the Father (see 3:22). He now tells us Jesus acted on his desire to tell as many of his fellow Jews as possible about the kingdom—about the possibility of accepting the same loving relationship with God he had accepted [v.44].

FIVE

Jesus Invites Others to Join Him in Bringing the Good News of Healing

JESUS CALLS SIMON AND OTHERS [LK.5:1–11]

¹ Once, [when he'd returned from traveling,] Jesus was teaching near Gennesaret on the lake, and the crowd kept pressing in to listen to the word of God. ² He saw two fishing boats beached there. The fishermen were on shore cleaning nets. ³ He got into Simon's boat, asked him to push out a bit, and sat in the boat to teach. ⁴ When he'd finished, he said, "Simon, row to deep water and put out your nets." ⁵ "We've worked all night, Master, to catch nothing. But, at your word, I'll cast nets." ⁶ They did this and caught so many fish the nets were breaking. ⁷ They had to get help from the other boat. The fish filled both boats to the point of sinking. ⁸ Simon Peter saw this, knelt to Jesus and said, "Leave me; I'm a sinner, Lord." ⁹ He and the others in his boat were astonished at their haul of fish. ¹⁰ So too were his partners in the other boat, James and John, the sons of Zebedee. Jesus said to Simon, "Don't fear. Now you'll net people." ¹¹ They beached their boats, left all behind, and followed him.

———❧❧❧———

Luke describes Jesus, back from a circuit of preaching (see 4:44), teaching south of Capernaum, near Gennesaret on the Lake of Galilee. He says Jesus first asked his friend Simon (see 4:38a) to loan him his boat as a pulpit; then told him to use the boat for fishing. Simon indulged both wishes of this traveling teacher ("Master") even though he said the second was pointless [vv.1–5]. He was surprised to find the Master knew more than he did [v.6]; then, in a few words, Luke depicts Simon's transformation from condescension to remorse [vv.7–8]. Next, he says Jesus urged Simon (also called Peter) and his partners in the fishing business not to fear. We hear them urged, instead, to look forward to doing exactly what Jesus had been doing: ensnaring listeners with the news that they are to share in God's kingdom [vv.9–10].

According to Luke, these men—who, a moment earlier, were dumbfounded by the results of Jesus' directions to them about catching fish—didn't hesitate to follow his direction to start captivating others with Good News [v.11]. The description of their swift, wordless response to Jesus' invitation contrasts with their first, fearful reaction to his display of power—a receptiveness that contrasts both with the skepticism Jesus met in Nazareth (see 4:28) and with the overbearing reaction of the crowds that pursued him and wondered at him (see 4:32, 36–37, 41, 42). Similar to Mary's response to the angel (see 1:38), their decisive action bespoke a simple "yes."

REACTION TO JESUS' HEALING IS TUMULTUOUS [LK.5:12–26]

[12] At another time, when Jesus was in a town by the lake, a leper saw him, bowed down, and begged, "Lord, if you want to, you can make me clean." [13] Jesus reached out his hand, touched him, and said, "I do want to. Be made clean." The leprosy instantly left him. [14] He told him not to talk about this. "But go," he said, "present yourself to the priest and give witness by making the offering prescribed by Moses" [see Lv.14:1–32]. [15] Nonetheless, talk about him increased, and crowds gathered to listen and be healed. [16] Meanwhile, Jesus kept going off to the wilderness to pray. [17] One day, when Pharisees and teachers of the Law from Galilee, Judea, and even Jerusalem came to hear him, the Lord's power to heal was with him. [18] Imagine, some men were trying to get a paralyzed man on a stretcher to Jesus. [19] But the crowd was so thick the men went to the

roof and lowered him over the tiles, into the courtyard in front of Jesus. [20] He saw their faith. He said to the paralyzed man, "Your sins are forgiven." [21] The scribes and Pharisees muttered, "This is blasphemy. Only God forgives sins!" [22] Jesus knew what they were thinking. He said, "What's in your hearts? [23] Is it easier to say, 'Your sins are forgiven,' or, 'Get up and walk'? [24] Watch how the Son of Man has power on earth to forgive sins: Get up," he said to the paralyzed man, "take your stretcher home." [25] Instantly, he got up, lifted the stretcher, and went to his house glorifying God. [26] All were filled with wonder. They too glorified God, saying, "What marvels!"

——◦◦◦——

Luke says Jesus told the leper not to talk to his neighbors about his luck, but to follow the Covenant's directions for celebrating a healing [vv.12–14]—directions that call for a sick person to repent of all sins and to testify to repentance through ritual actions. But the leper healed by Jesus, rather than giving witness to his belief in God's healing love, apparently chose to speak about his cure simply as news [v.15]. Luke contrasts the frantic reaction to this news with Jesus' impulse to keep calling upon God's caring presence in quiet, private prayer [v.16].

Next, Luke tells us influential religious teachers accused Jesus of blasphemy when he responded to a bold appeal for healing by saying a man's sins were forgiven [vv.19–21]. The Jesus whom Luke has described to us so far in this Gospel is someone who trusts completely in the generosity and graciousness of God, and here we see Jesus again turning to the Father [v.16]. Earlier, we saw how the Father was delighted when Jesus turned to him (see 3:22). Though Luke has consistently portrayed Jesus, a Son of Man—that is, a human being—turning to God for inspiration and receiving it, he's also told us that Jesus' neighbors in Nazareth couldn't imagine how such a relationship could have developed (see 4:16–30). Here, it's religious experts who can't imagine how Jesus, a man, can express and share complete acceptance of God's mercy. Luke says Jesus asked these teachers why their hearts harbored doubt rather than trust in God's desire to give us his Spirit and to console us with healing and forgiveness [vv.22–25]. He adds that the crowd praised God—though they were surprised by what they'd seen and heard [v.26].

JESUS INVITES A SINNER TO FOLLOW HIM; HE DEFENDS REJOICING [LK.5:27–39]

[27] *Leaving [the teachers of the Law (see 5:17)], Jesus noticed Levi, a tariff collector, sitting at his post. He said, "Follow me."* [28] *He got up, left his post, and followed him.* [29] *At home, Levi set a feast for him at which many fee collectors and others reclined.* [30] *The Pharisees and their scribes saw this and complained to his disciples, "Why do you eat with tariff takers and sinners?"* [31] *It was Jesus who answered, "The healthy don't need physicians, but the sick do.* [32] *I haven't come to call the righteous to repentance, but sinners."* [33] *They said, "John's disciples and the Pharisees' pupils fast and pray; yours feast."* [34] *He asked them, "Can you make the groomsmen fast while he's celebrating with them?* [35] *The time will come when he's taken from them. They can fast then."* [36] *He offered a parable: "No one cuts a piece of material from a new cloak to patch an old one. That would ruin the new without patching the old.* [37] *And no one pours new wine into old skins—bursting the old and spilling the new.* [38] *New wine is poured into new wineskins.* [39] *Those who like old wine won't try new. They say, 'The old is good enough.'"*

——❦——

According to Luke, Jesus' invitation to Levi [v.27] not only prompted a swifter response than Simon's (see 5:8–11), but also inspired Levi to celebrate his invitation by feasting with old cronies [v.29]—something that disturbed protectors of the Law (Pharisees) and legal specialists (scribes), who saw Jesus at the feast [v.30]. Luke's description of Jesus' answer to their question has no hint of indignation—not even at the fact that it was muttered to his disciples. It simply notes that those in perfect shape don't need the blessings of healing, and those who feel completely righteous don't seek the joys of repentance [vv.31–32].

Luke then says these scholars of the Law wondered why Jesus let his disciples feast if he was trying to teach them repentance [v.33]. The answer Luke reports suggests that Jesus (like Levi) thought that hearing the call to repentance and accepting the Good News about God's kingdom were reasons to rejoice [v.34]. When Jesus was gone and his words began to be forgotten, that would be the time for his disciples to fast—that is, to turn away from any selfish concerns (including anxiety about food) and to recall Jesus' message [v.35]. Luke says Jesus then offered some simple images to suggest how foolish it is to pick up something new but pretend it's the same as something old. This is a clear appeal to the Pharisees and scribes to listen to him without insisting that his words should express the same (old) thoughts they have in their heads. But Luke describes them as huffy and censorious, not at all willing to listen to Jesus. So it's not obvious to them that they're misapplying the Law to his message. They're like a curmudgeon who says no to anything new [vv.36–39].

SIX

Jesus Discusses the Law and Explains Its Implications

WHAT IS THE LAW OF GOD? [LK.6:1–11]

¹ Once, on a Sabbath, as Jesus went through a grain field, his disciples plucked kernels, cracked them in their hands, and ate them. ² Some Pharisees complained, "Why do you do what's unlawful on the Sabbath?" ³ Jesus said, "Haven't you read what David did when he and his men were hungry? ⁴ He entered God's house with his men and ate the offering loaves reserved for priests. ⁵ The Son of Man is the Lord of the Sabbath," he explained. ⁶ On another Sabbath he taught in a synagogue where a man had a maimed hand. ⁷ Some scribes and Pharisees watched, hoping to accuse him of healing on a Sabbath. ⁸ Knowing their thoughts, he said to the maimed man, "Stand up front." He did. ⁹ Jesus asked them, "Is it lawful on a Sabbath to do good, or evil; save life, or end it?" ¹⁰ He gazed at them. Then he said, "Spread your hand." The man did. It was healed. ¹¹ They were crazed with rage. They talked of doing something to him.

———✦✦✦———

Luke says casual snacking on a Sabbath provoked another complaint from legal scholars [vv.1–2] who seem more ready to judge than to learn (see 5:30, 33). But we read that Jesus cited scripture (see 1 Sm.21:1–6) to help them reimagine their notion of the Law. If David could put a pressing need for food above a ritual regulation [vv.3–4], perhaps the disciples' hunger can excuse them from the Sabbath law against labor—that is, perhaps the Law doesn't call merely for rote compliance. Luke says Jesus addressed an implicit question (What *does* the Law call for?) by saying the Son of Man was Lord of the Sabbath. From Luke's point of view, Jesus is the Son of Man who is the perfect Lord of the Sabbath because he puts his complete trust in God (see 3:22). But every son of man—every human being—is invited to hear the Law's call to trust; to see, as Jesus does, that the purpose of the Sabbath rest is to free us from any concern other than rejoicing in God's care for us [v.5]. Perfect trust, not slavish conformity to the Law, makes Jesus, and anyone who follows him, Lord of the Sabbath.

According to Luke, this lesson didn't move the legalists. They waited for another Sabbath to trap Jesus [vv.6–7]. But, says Luke, Jesus still tried to teach them that, if they cling only to the letter of the Law, they'll forget that the purpose of all the Lord's commands is to bring life (see Dt.30:15–16). Luke says Jesus tried to show them what he meant by telling the maimed man to let life flow back into his hand [vv.8–10]. This manifestation of God's care for us—his power to heal and make us whole—produced heat, not light, in the scholars of the Law [v.11].

JESUS ASKS TWELVE TO SHARE HIS MISSION, THEN DEMONSTRATES IT [LK.6:12–19]

[12] *Once, Jesus went to the heights above Capernaum to spend the night praying to God.* [13] *At dawn, he called his disciples and chose twelve of them to be "apostles."* [14] *They were Simon (whom he called Peter) and Andrew, his brother, James, John, Philip, Bartholomew,* [15] *Matthew, Thomas, James-son-of-Alphaeus, Simon "the Zealot,"* [16] *Judas-son-of-James, and Judas Iscariot who became a traitor.* [17] *Then he came down with them to open country, meeting a great crowd of his disciples and people from all over Judea and Jerusalem, even from Tyre and Sidon on the coast.* [18] *They came to hear him and to be healed. Even*

the bedeviled were healed. ¹⁹ *Everyone wanted to touch him because divine power came through him, healing.*

———⟿⟿⟿———

Just above, Luke recounted two incidents in which Jesus tried to teach other teachers the need to trust God's goodness rather than their own sense of what's right. Here he shows us Jesus practicing what he preached: turning to God [v.12]. Placing Jesus on the cliffs west of the Lake of Galilee, Luke says he told twelve of his disciples he wanted them to work as his "apostles"—that is, to accept the responsibility of being "sent" or "commissioned" by him to do the same work he'd been doing [v.13].

Earlier, Luke promised to speak of "all matters" important to Jesus' teaching (see 1:1), but now he says nothing about Jesus' reasons for choosing these twelve [vv.14–16]. There's no hint that Jesus wanted to remind his disciples of the twelve tribes of Israel (see below, 22:30), or that he thought thirteen was a good number for a group of itinerants, or that he liked these disciples more than others. What seems important to Luke here is to point out that Jesus wanted certain disciples to act directly on his behalf. They would, of course, need to learn how to act, and Luke describes Jesus teaching them by example: he responds to people's need to be freed from afflictions and torments [vv.17–18]. He does this by trusting in God's power to renew us and make us whole, and by allowing that power to be shared with those who seek it [v.19].

Next, Luke will describe Jesus explaining how God works to fill all of us with his power.

JESUS TEACHES HOW TO ACCEPT GOD'S BLESSINGS
[LK.6:20–38]

²⁰ *Jesus looked at his disciples and said, "Blessed are you poor; yours is the kingdom of God.* ²¹ *Happy are you who hunger now; you'll be filled. Happy are you who weep now; you'll laugh.* ²² *Happy are you when people hate you, reject you, ridicule you, and call you evil—all because of the Son of Man.* ²³ *Rejoice that*

day. Leap for joy. Look, your great reward is in heaven. (Their ancestors treated the prophets the same way!) ²⁴ But woe to you rich. Your consolation has already come. ²⁵ Woe to you well-fed; you will be hungry. Woe, you laughers; you will grieve and weep. ²⁶ Woe is yours when all praise you. (Their ancestors praised the false prophets.) ²⁷ Now listen: Love your enemies; do good to those who hate you. ²⁸ Bless those who curse you. Pray for those who bully you. ²⁹ If someone hits your cheek, offer the other. If they take your cloak, give your shirt. ³⁰ Give to everyone who asks. Don't demand things back from filchers. ³¹ What you want others to do to you, you do to them. ³² If you love those who love you, so what? Even sinners love those who love them. ³³ If you're good to those who are good to you, so what? Sinners do that much. ³⁴ If you lend only for a return, so what? Sinners lend to sinners and get a return. ³⁵ So, love your enemies. Serve and lend, getting nothing back. ³⁶ Be merciful—just as your Father is merciful. ³⁷ Don't judge, and you won't be judged; don't condemn, and you won't be condemned. Forgive, and you'll be forgiven. ³⁸ Give, then you'll get gifts—an ample measure pressed together, shaken tight, and tumbling off your lap. How you measure out will be the measure used on you."

As Luke describes them, the blessings and burdens Jesus lists for his disciples are simple. If, for instance, you're hungry, eating is likely to be in your future; if you're stuffed, you'll get hungry again. But Luke doesn't present this as a motivational speech. Jesus isn't simply telling the disciples to take life's lumps along with its pleasures. The first assertion, "Happy are the poor!" seems intended to stun, as does the summary blessing which assures those who follow Jesus that they'll be blessed with hatred, rejection, ridicule, and condemnation, while rich, well-fed, self-satisfied celebrities will, at worst, experience a sense of longing despite their comforts and adulation [vv.20–26]. Which of us wants poverty, hatred, rejection, and ridicule? Who doesn't like wealth and flattery?

Wait; there's more! Are you willing to respond to hate with love—to give kindness to bullies, to be generous with cheats, and to see only yourself in others and treat them accordingly [vv.27–31]? Luke says Jesus described those without this love as mere combatants in a ceaseless war of competing interests [vv.32–34]. Then, after repeating the command to love enemies [v.35a], we hear Jesus remind his disciples where they are to get this gift of patient love: from God, their Father, who is passionate about sharing the power of forgiving [vv.35b–36]. Jesus tells his disciples that, if they want to be as gracious as God, they must first notice their temptation to judge; then they must choose to forgive, not judge. When they give up their hasty opinions about others, they'll experience forgiveness and an overwhelming sense of happiness [vv.37–38].

JESUS' DISCIPLES MUST LEARN FORGIVENESS—AND KEEP LEARNING IT [LK.6:39–49]

[39] *He told a parable. "If a blind person leads a blind person, won't both fall in a hole?* [40] *A student isn't above the teacher. After training, a student becomes like the teacher.* [41] *Can you see a speck in someone's eye, but not the log in your own?* [42] *How can you say, 'Let me get that speck for you,' if you're blind from a beam? You phony! Take the log out of your eye! Then you might help with that speck.* [43] *A healthy tree doesn't produce bad fruit, nor does a sick tree give good fruit.* [44] *You tell a plant by its fruit. You find no figs on brambles, no grapes on thistles.* [45] *The good, from the goodly riches of their hearts, bring good. The evil, from evil hearts, bring evil. The mouth speaks of what fills the heart.* [46] *Why call me, 'Lord, Lord,' and not do as I say?* [47] *I'll tell you what it's like to come to me: listen to my words, and act on them.* [48] *That would be like the house builder who dug a deep foundation into rock. When a flood hurled a river against that house, it wasn't shaken because it was well built.* [49] *But the listener who doesn't act on my words is like a builder who lays no foundation—whose house the river rushes over and tears completely down."*

—————

Luke says Jesus used farcical images of blind guides, impudent students, and lumber-loaded eyes to ridicule pride [vv.39–42]. Then we hear Jesus point out the difference between complacency and kindness—a difference as easy to recognize as it is to tell blighted crops from wholesome fruit. It's as plain as noticing that figs don't grow on a thorn bush and grapes don't sprout from .prickly weeds [vv.43–44]. Luke adds that Jesus told his disciples they could recognize what choices their hearts were making by noting what they talked about [v.45].

Then, says Luke, Jesus ended this lesson with his disciples by asking them whether or not they truly desired to learn forgiveness. Were they like the audience that fawns over a speaker after a lecture, but then forgets what was said [v.46]? According to Luke, Jesus told his disciples that, if they wanted to know whether or not they were taking him seriously about the challenges of forgiving, they should ask if they were like a home builder who not only chooses a site for a house but also pays attention to the demands of that site [vv.47–49]. Or are they like the builder who simply thinks, "I like this spot; I'll settle here" [vv.47–49]?

SEVEN

Healing, and What It Means

A ROMAN OFFICER ASKS JESUS TO HEAL A SLAVE [LK.7:1–10]

¹ After Jesus finished speaking [see 6:20ff.], he went back to Capernaum. ² A centurion stationed there had a favorite slave who was sick, nearing death. ³ Having heard of Jesus, he asked Jewish elders to ask him to heal his slave. ⁴ They went to Jesus and asked, "Please, it's right to do this for him. ⁵ He respects our nation. He built the synagogue for us." ⁶ Jesus went with them and wasn't far from the house when the centurion sent friends to say, "Lord, trouble yourself no more. It's not fitting you should come under my roof. ⁷ Neither was it proper to come to you myself. Say the word, my slave will be healed. ⁸ I know how to follow orders, and my soldiers must follow mine. I tell one, 'Go,' he goes; I say, 'Come,' the other comes; I tell my slave, 'Do this,' and he does." ⁹ Jesus, wondering at the man, said, "I can't say I've found faith like this in Israel." ¹⁰ When the friends sent by the centurion returned, they found the slave well.

—————

After just reporting Jesus' lessons about God's gifts, here Luke describes a plea from a non-Jew for the gift of healing. Although the need described is urgent [v.2], the officer's appeal isn't peremptory. It's made with great courtesy. Luke portrays the man as so sensitive to the proper use of power that he sent friends [v.6] to explain that

41

his reason for not imposing on Jesus personally, or bringing him into his house, was a sense of respect [vv.6b–7a]. This man's reluctance to use his position to demand a favor stands in contrast with the elders' anxious insistence on the man's worthiness [vv.3–5].

Luke tells us the centurion followed the rules governing the social contract between himself, a Roman officer, and Jesus, a Jewish teacher, because he believed those rules were effective [vv.6–8]—a belief that had apparently led him to trust that the Law followed by Jesus was also effective. We're told his experience as an officer had convinced him his soldiers and servants would do what he told them—he'd learned how people behave who trust in a particular relationship. So, apparently, when he heard that Jesus put his confidence in a God who offers reconciliation and healing, he chose to share Jesus' trust in that relationship. Luke tells us Jesus marveled that no one he'd met so far in Israel had chosen to trust in God as confidently as this man had [v.9]. Then we hear the centurion's messengers were received back home with the good news that the beloved slave had returned to health [v.10].

JESUS IS MOVED WITH PITY FOR A WIDOW AND HER DEAD SON [LK.7:11–17]

[11] Jesus traveled south to the town of Nain accompanied by disciples and a crowd. [12] As he approached the town gate, a dead man was being carried out on a litter. He was a widow's only son. A great crowd from the town was with the widow. [13] The Lord saw her and had pity. He said, "Don't cry." [14] He went up and touched the litter, and the bearers stopped. "Young man," he said, "I tell you to get up." [15] The dead man sat up and began to speak. He gave him back to his mother. [16] Everyone was startled. But they glorified God: "A great prophet has been raised up!" and, "God has visited his people!" [17] Reports of this excitement spread south into Judea and all around Galilee.

———✽✽✽———

Luke's description of Jesus' pity and the miracle that flows from it may remind readers of the story about Elijah pleading with God to hear his appeal for help, then raising the recently deceased son of a widow (see 1 Kgs.17:17–24). Above, Luke said Jesus was struck with wonder by a centurion's appeal for help and his trust in God's compassion. Here, he tells us Jesus allowed himself to be filled with divine compassion in response to the plight of a widow [vv.11–13]. By acting on this compassion and telling the widow's son to rise [v.14], Jesus was following the very command that he'd given to his disciples to act with God's kindness (see 6:36). Anyone who reads about this return from the dead may feel the same astonishment that Luke attributes to all the people (including the disciples) who witnessed it [v.16a]. And yet, if we imagine that the disciples mentioned in this scene had also been present to hear what Jesus taught about God's blessings (see 6:20–25), and if we suppose they believed that teaching, we may wonder why they were astonished when Jesus' pity for a widow's distress revealed that the merciful blessings of God are real. Is Luke hinting that the disciples, unlike Jesus, hadn't yet let themselves be filled with God's gifts of mercy, forgiveness, and love?

We're told by Luke the crowds in this scene were surprised into praise; that they testified that God was in their presence in the person of a mighty prophet [v.16]. Then they reported their experience in every direction [v.17]. As they spread their report, do you suppose they emphasized their trust in God's healing presence among us? Or did they share their shock at witnessing that presence?

JOHN THE BAPTIST'S DISCIPLES ASK ABOUT EXPECTATIONS; JESUS ANSWERS [LK.7:18–28]

[18] When John's disciples told him these reports [see 7:17], he sent off two of them. [19] They were to ask Jesus, "Are you the one who is coming, or should we look for another?" [20] They went and said, "John the Baptist sent us to ask if you're the one coming." [21] Jesus was freeing many from ills, hurts, and demons, and giving sight to the blind. [22] He said, "Tell John what you've seen and heard: the blind see, cripples walk, lepers are cleansed, the deaf hear, the dead are raised, and the poor are told Good News. [23] How happy is the one who's not

tripped up by me." ²⁴ When John's messengers left, Jesus asked the crowd
around him, "What did you go out to the wilderness to see, a reed waving in the
wind? ²⁵ What then? A man in fine clothes? That sort lives in a palace. ²⁶ What
then? A prophet? Yes! But I say: more than that. ²⁷ Scripture speaks of him:
'Look, I send my messenger ahead to prepare your way.' ²⁸ It's true, no one
human-born is greater than John. And yet, the least in God's kingdom is greater
than he."

————•◦•————

Luke doesn't explain why John (still in prison—see 3:20) sent disciples to ask if Jesus was the one whose coming he'd expected (see
3:16). We can suppose he was uncertain about Jesus, or that he
wanted these students to find their own answers about "reports"
[vv.18–19]. When they approach Jesus (Luke doesn't say where)
[vv.20–21], he tells them, first, to note what they see and, second, to
notice their response—that is, they see healing brought to the distressed and Good News proclaimed to the poor (see 6:20), and they
should notice whether they're buoyed or troubled by this. If they
feel uplifted—like the poor, sick, and bedeviled who rejoice in healing—they are also being filled with the joy that comes from God
[vv.22–23].

Then, says Luke, Jesus asked the crowd to reflect on their expectations. Had they sought to see John because of idle curiosity [v.24]?
Had they hoped to meet a noble personage [v.25]? Or had they
hoped to be moved by a prophetic message? Yes, says Jesus, John,
like other prophets, proclaimed the rightness of repentance
[v.26a]—that is, he announced that God's people should turn to
God and receive his care (see Ex.20:2–3). But Luke describes Jesus
saying that John, like the prophet Malachi (see Mal.3:1), also proclaimed that a messenger was coming to fulfill God's promise of
care [v.27]. Then, says Luke, Jesus asked the crowd to think, first, of
John who received great praise from this world; second, of the least
nobody who receives the kingdom of God. The nonentity is pro-
nounced to have the greater joy [v.28]. This is the joy Jesus is shar-

ing with the sick, the needy, and with sinners. Did John's disciples feel that joy? Did the crowd? Did they expect to?

MORE ABOUT EXPECTATIONS [LK.7:29–35]

[29] Even such sinners as tariff collectors celebrated John's baptism of renewal and accepted God's way as right. [30] But some Pharisees and legal scholars rejected baptism and God's plan for them. [31] Jesus asked the crowd [see 7:24], "To what shall I compare this generation? They're like—what? [32] They're like children at the market who complain, 'We piped, but you wouldn't dance; we wailed, but you wouldn't weep.' [33] John the Baptist came to you fasting and abstaining, and you said he had a demon. [34] The Son of Man came to you eating and drinking, and you say, 'Look! A glutton! A drunk! A friend of the tariff collectors—of sinners!' [35] The rightness of Wisdom is made obvious by all her children."

—◦◦◦—

Luke reminds us that, in response to John's call for repentance, many people recognized their selfishness, turned away from sinning, and proclaimed through baptism their desire to be immersed in God rather than themselves [v.29]. He also notes that many students of the Law, who should have known about the Covenant's call for repentance, rejected this call when it came from John [v.30]. Then Luke tells us Jesus compared this perversity to the contrariness of spoiled children [vv.31–32]. What an irony that these adults—who are also serious scholars—behave like children who can't imagine why others don't share their desires and meet their expectations: "If we want to dance, so should you; if we ululate, you should join us." Although these students of the Law would probably tell their children, if they behaved this way, to stop whining and find a game everyone could play, they seem blind to their own stubbornly self-indulgent behavior.

Because of this blindness, says Jesus, they can't see how ridiculous it is for them to cry out against any call for repentance—whether it seemed austere or looked like fun [vv.33–34]. Luke tells us that, to these self-confident scholars, Jesus offered an implicit invitation to open their minds to the possibility they were wrong. Watch, he says: "Wait for a while and see if the choice that I, John, and others have taught—that is, to turn to God—begins to look like the right choice, the wise choice. Those who put all their trust in God will be seen to be growing in wisdom; they will be recognized as children of wisdom" [v.35].

REPENTANCE SEEKS FORGIVENESS [LK.7:36–50]

[36] *When a Pharisee invited Jesus to dinner, he went and reclined at table.* [37] *Imagine, a woman known as a sinner in that town heard where he was dining, bought an alabaster vial of fragrant ointment, and brought it to the house.* [38] *She stood at his feet, weeping. Raining tears on his feet, she wiped them with her hair, kissed them, and rubbed them with the pungent oil.* [39] *When his host, the Pharisee, saw this, he thought, "If this one were a prophet, he'd know what sort of woman was touching him—he'd know she was a sinner!"* [40] *"Simon," said Jesus, "I have something to say." "Say it, Teacher," he said.* [41] *"Once, a creditor had two debtors, one owing five hundred silver coins, another fifty.* [42] *When they couldn't pay, he forgave both debts. Which will love him more?"* [43] *"I guess," he said, "the one who owed more." "Good guess," said Jesus.* [44] *"See this woman, Simon? When I came to your house, you didn't bathe my feet, but she splashed them with her tears and wiped them with her hair.* [45] *You greeted me with no kiss, but, as soon as I reclined, she kept kissing my feet.* [46] *You offered no balm for my head. She, however, rubbed my feet with fragrant oil.* [47] *I tell you this: after seeing that her great numbers of sins were forgiven, she loved greatly. The one who sees little need for forgiveness sees little need for love."* [48] *He told her, "Your sins are forgiven."* [49] *Those reclining at table with him said, "Who's he to forgive sins?"* [50] *But he said to the woman, "It's your faith that brings salvation. Go in peace."*

———

After recounting Jesus' address to his disciples about living by God's law (see 6:20–49), Luke described how healing came to someone who trusted God's desire to give it (see 7:9); how God's compassion was life giving (see 7:14); how repentance and reconciliation brought us to God's kingdom (see 7:28); and how foolish it was not to turn to God (see 7:32). Here, Luke tells a story that depicts both the disgruntled attitude of unrepentant individuals and the joy of the penitent sinner.

A penitent woman, whose sins aren't specified, is pictured as so eager to be relieved of her burden of guilt that she braves the judgment of others to meet Jesus, the healer [vv.37–38]. The host Pharisee is described as swift to judge [v.39]. We hear Jesus helping Simon, his host, reimagine what happens when someone who needs forgiveness realizes that the person is willing to give it [vv.40–43]. We also hear him note that Simon's welcome was less effusive than the woman's [vv.44–46]. The woman behaved as she did, says Jesus, because she realized that her appeal for relief was not going to be rejected. And her hope for the possibility of reconciliation was rewarded [v.47]. Luke says Jesus' willingness to let the woman approach him filled his host with dismay but overwhelmed the woman with gratitude and love. Luke adds that Jesus further shocked the judgmental guests at the dinner by telling the woman she was forgiven [vv.48–49]—a grace-filled condition she reached because she believed it could be given to her [v.50].

EIGHT

Jesus Travels, Teaches, and Heals

¹ Jesus traveled from one town and village to the next, proclaiming the Good News of the kingdom of God. With him were the twelve, ² and women who'd been healed of demons and diseases. There was Mary from Magdala, from whom seven demons had fled. ³ There was Joanna, wife of Chuza, Herod's steward. And there were many others who gave assistance with whatever means they had at their disposal. ⁴ Once, when a crowd had gathered from various towns, he told a parable. ⁵ "A sower went out sowing, and dropped seeds on a path where they were crushed or eaten by birds. ⁶ Other seeds fell on gravel, sprang up, but withered without moisture. ⁷ Others fell among thorns, grew, but were smothered by the thorns. ⁸ Others fell on good soil, grew, and yielded hundreds more seeds." He then cried, "Let everyone with ears hear." ⁹ The disciples asked what the parable meant. ¹⁰ "You've been given knowledge about the mysteries of God's kingdom. The rest are given parables; as it says: 'they look but don't see, hear but don't absorb' [Is.6:9]."

———❧❧❧———

Does Luke want us to see the disciples as truly knowledgeable [v.10]—and, if so, why does he describe them asking for an explanation of the parable [v.9]? Anyone putting this scene on film would

49

have to decide whether or not Jesus' description of the disciples' knowledge about the mysteries of God's kingdom might be expressed ironically—an irony that would be deepened, first, by Jesus' assertion that the parable was comprehensible to anyone with ears [v.8b], and, second, by the citation from the Book of Isaiah expressing frustration with people's slowness to take in God's word [v.10].

The parable focuses on the fact that a seed's power to be fruitful is so great that, though any sown seed may be wasted, nonetheless any single seed is able to produce a bountiful harvest [vv.4–8a]. Luke has told us that the audience for this parable included the twelve disciples whom Jesus specifically commissioned to join him in his work (see 6:13), plus many female disciples who'd experienced healing [vv.1–3]. Unlike individuals in the gathered crowd that might have been hearing the Good News for the first time, Jesus' disciples have by now heard repeatedly about healing, forgiveness, and reconciliation. They have heard that the promise proclaimed by scripture—the promise of God's mercy and love—is being fulfilled right now. Yes, right now the kingdom of God welcomes anyone who wants to enter it (see 7:28). The disciples described here by Luke seem to need to hear this message again. So it shouldn't surprise us to read below that Jesus tells them the message again.

JESUS PRODS HIS LISTENERS TO TRUST GOD'S WORD
[LK.8:11–21]

[11] "This," said Jesus, "is what the parable means: the seed is God's Word. [12] On the path are those who hear it, but the devil takes it before belief can save them. [13] In the gravel are joyful hearers who form no roots. They collapse in adversity. [14] In the thorns are hearers who, distracted by worries, wealth, and lust, bear no fruit. [15] In the rich soil, the word is taken into good, generous hearts where patience allows it to bear fruit. [16] No one lights a lamp to put it under a pot or a bed, but on a stand so all can see. [17] Nothing's hidden that won't be disclosed, nothing's secret that won't be told. [18] Notice how you listen. Those who have will

get more. Those who don't have will find the nothing they have taken away."
¹⁹ His mother and brothers approached but couldn't reach him because of the
crowd. ²⁰ "Your mother and brothers are out there," they said. "They want to see
you." ²¹ "My mother and brothers are those who hear the word of God and do it,"
he said.

———《》———

Jesus' comment above to his disciples about parables (see 8:10) suggests that, if they can't grasp a simple story—a parable—about God,
perhaps they still have much to learn about God. So, says Luke,
Jesus taught them. He told them to think of God's word—the promises and commands found in scripture—as a seed that's ineffective
unless it's taken in, savored, and given time to grow. Those who
don't cherish God's word will have it snatched away before it can
free them from their cares [v.12]. Those who won't let it affect them
deeply, or are obsessed with other concerns, will let it come to nothing [vv.13–14]. But imagine the empty heart that lets itself fill up
with God's word—with understanding of God's desires and
dreams [v.15].

Then, says Luke, Jesus used a few homely images to describe the
kind of attention God's word requires. God's word is like a lamp.
Because you need it to help you see, you don't put it where it can't
give constant light [v.16]. It's like a secret. Just wait; it will come out
[v.17]. If you are listening for this word, your awareness of it will
increase—like noticing an itch. If you never notice it, it fades to
meaningless background noise [v.18].

Luke says that, when Jesus' family showed up in the midst of
this lesson about God's word, Jesus challenged the crowd's assumption that this arrival of relatives would demand his complete attention. Luke tells us Jesus pointed out that attention to the word of
God was the pressing need that could unite all of us more closely
than blood or family ties [vv.19–21].

A LAKE CROSSING REVEALS A LACK OF FAITH [LK.8:22–26]

²² One day, Jesus boarded a boat with his disciples, saying, "Let's cross the lake." Off they went. ²³ Once under sail, he fell asleep. A sudden squall hit, threatening to swamp them. ²⁴ They went to wake him: "Master, Master, we're dead!" He woke up, commanded the wind and raging water, which died down to calm. ²⁵ "Where's your faith?" he asked. They were stunned. "Who can this be?" they asked one another. "He commands even the water and winds. They obey him!" ²⁶ They sailed on to Gerasene territory, on the opposite side of the lake from Galilee.

———◦◦◦———

Just above (8:18, 21), Luke described Jesus telling his disciples to behave as if the Good News was true—as if God's promise of care and concern for them was trustworthy. Now we hear how difficult it is to do that. Here, at first, the disciples respond to Jesus' word with the same alacrity and trust shown by Simon Peter and others when Jesus first called them (see 5:11, 28). No one says, for instance, "But that's heading toward Gentile territory!" When asked, they simply joined Jesus on this trip [v.22].

The moment of quiet compliance with Jesus' directions suddenly ended, says Luke, when the weather changed [v.23]. All at once, the disciples regretted being on the lake. We can imagine the disciples' horror of immanent capsizing. We can also imagine that Jesus' ability to sleep, remaining peacefully unaware of peril, may have added to their sense of dismay. How could he not realize the danger they faced? Luke reports that Jesus responded to their hysterical cries [v.24] but then asked them why they hadn't put their trust in God (as he did). He says the disciples were astonished at Jesus' response to the raging winds and waves [v.25], and they didn't know how to answer their own questions about Jesus: who exactly was he, and how did he have such power? Jesus gave them the answer to their questions about his identity when he asked them, "Where's your faith?" That question told them who he was. In effect, he was saying, "I trust the Father completely; my power is the Father's power.

After all, if you put your faith in a God who wants to fill you with divine power and glory (see, e.g., 1:35; 2:49; 3:22), what expectation would you have, but that God would actually give you that power and glory?" According to Luke, Jesus wanted his disciples to have the same expectation—an expectation they had plenty of time to mull over as they completed their crossing [v.26].

MOST GERASENES REJECT THE GOOD NEWS; ONE PROCLAIMS IT [LK.8:27–39]

27 When Jesus landed in Gerasene territory, a bedeviled man met him. The man had long lurked outside the town, naked and homeless among the seaside tombs. 28 He saw Jesus, shrieked, fell before him. And a big voice said: "What's with you and me, Jesus, son of God Most High? Stop badgering me." 29 (Jesus had been ordering it out. It had often driven the man to break his restraints, elude his guards, and run into the wilderness.) 30 "What's your name?" asked Jesus. "Legion." Many demons had gone into him; 31 and they begged Jesus not to send them into the abyss [the devil's prison]. 32 They begged to be allowed to enter the pigs rooting in the hills. He let them. 33 The demons left the man, entered the pigs, and the pigs ran into the lake and drowned. 34 Pig keepers saw this and ran through the town and the countryside telling this news. 35 Those who were curious came out and saw the man at Jesus' feet. He was dressed and lucid. They were afraid. 36 The witnesses told the curious onlookers how the bedeviled man had been healed. 37 But the Gerasenes were so frightened they asked Jesus to leave. So, he embarked. 38 The man freed from demons wanted to stay with Jesus, but he gave him a commission. 39 "Go home and tell everything God did for you." He went and told the town what Jesus did.

―――⟳⟳⟳―――

Although Luke has described the effects of Jesus' teaching primarily on the Jews of Judea and Galilee (see 4:44; 5:17; 6:17; 7:17), he's also mentioned its influence in Gentile areas (see 6:17; 7:9). He may therefore have felt no need to explain Jesus' decision to visit a Gentile area so near Galilee. Word of Jesus' healing powers seems to have reached this territory, for Luke says Jesus had just landed when a deeply troubled man flung himself at him, but then begged not to be touched by Jesus' power [vv.27–28]. Jesus' immediate impulse was to free the man from bedevilment [v.29a]. The fellow's condition and history were obvious [v.29b].

Luke says Jesus answered the man's request to leave him alone by asking his name. Instead of getting an answer from the man, the disturbing presence spoke, claiming to be "a multitude." Then the presence asked Jesus for a favor: "Please don't render us harmless; let us bedevil those pigs"—a plea Jesus granted [vv.30–32], thereby revealing the self-destructive nature of the spirits [v.33]. Luke says these events were broadly reported, but the reaction of those who came to verify them was fear [vv.34–35]. According to Luke, even when eyewitnesses pointed out that the man had been saved from the destructive forces within him [v.36], people of that region chose to fear rather than rejoice. They asked to be freed from Jesus' presence, and Jesus granted their wish [v.37]. On the other hand, we hear that the man who was freed from deadly evils asked if he could go with Jesus. Luke tells us Jesus sent him instead to tell his neighbors the whole story of what had happened to him—a mission the man accepted [vv.38–39].

TWO PEOPLE SEEK HEALING, AND RECEIVE IT [LK.8:40–56]

[40] A crowd waited to meet Jesus upon his return from Gerasene territory. [41] Imagine, Jairus, a synagogue leader, came up, fell at Jesus' feet and begged him to come to his house. [42] His only daughter, about twelve, was dying. As Jesus went with Jairus, the crowds pressed in. [43] There was a woman who'd hemorrhaged for twelve years, wasting money on quacks. [44] She came up behind him, touched the fringe of his cloak, and the bleeding stopped. [45] "Who touched me?" he asked. No one admitted it, and Peter said, "It's crowded." [46] "Someone touched me. I know power has gone out of me." [47] The woman saw she'd been noticed, trembled, fell before him, and said she'd touched him and had found instant healing. [48] "Your faith has saved you, daughter," he said. "Go in peace." [49] As he spoke, someone from the synagogue leader's house came up and said, "Your daughter has died. Trouble the Teacher no further." [50] "Don't be afraid,"

said Jesus when he heard this. "Have faith and she'll be saved." [51] At the house, he let no one in with him but Peter, James, John and the parents. [52] He said to those weeping and wailing, "Don't weep. She's not dead, but asleep." [53] They laughed at this because they knew she was dead. [54] Then he took her hand and said, "Little one, get up." [55] Her breath returned. She got up immediately. He told them to give her some food. [56] Her parents were amazed. He told them not to tell others what had happened.

⟞⟋∿⟍⟝

Luke says the crowd waiting for Jesus' return allowed Jairus to present his need. Then they eagerly went along to see the outcome [vv.40–42]. Next, Luke introduces someone whose desperation drove her to approach Jesus, though not to speak [vv.43–44]. Luke has presented Jesus as concerned only with the Father's work, and here he says Jesus was instantly aware that God's power had worked through him [v.46]. All except the woman were unaware of this power—including Peter [v.45]. The woman who felt the effects of the power confessed as much with some reluctance [v.47]. But Jesus told her to be peaceful. Her frustration with all her own efforts to find healing had led her to put faith in God [v.48].

Next, we hear Jairus told to give up hope [v.49]. But he was told the opposite by Jesus: "Keep believing in God's power" [v.50]. Luke says Jesus chose five individuals who may have seemed ready to believe. He took them away from the grieving crowd that ridiculed belief [vv.51–53]. Jesus then acted on the belief he'd been teaching others to embrace. He told the child to rise and return to the activities of this life, such as eating [vv.54–55]. Luke tells us the parents were amazed, suggesting they hadn't really believed. Unlike the Gerasene man, they don't ask to follow Jesus. So Jesus asks them not to proclaim the Good News. They don't seem ready to do that [v.56].

NINE

What It Means to Follow Jesus

JESUS SENDS OUT THE TWELVE WHOM HE COMMISSIONED
[LK.9:1–9]

[1] Jesus called the twelve together and gave them power over demons and authority to cure diseases. [2] Then he sent them to proclaim the kingdom of God and to heal. [3] He said, "Take nothing on the road—no staff, bag, bread, or coins; no second shirt. [4] When you stay at a house, work from there. [5] If you're not welcomed, leave the town, knocking its dust from your feet as a sign." [6] They went from town to town, proclaiming the Good News and healing. [7] Herod the Tetrarch heard what was happening and was puzzled because some people were saying John was risen from the dead. [8] Others said Elijah had appeared. Some said an ancient prophet had reappeared. [9] "I beheaded John," said Herod. "Who's this I hear about?" He wanted to see him.

———❧❧❧———

We've been told Jesus let twelve of his disciples know he had a mission for them (see 6:13). Here, we see them given the power to carry out that mission—the work of freeing the bedeviled from their demons, healing the sick [v.1], and announcing that God's kingdom brings wholeness and well-being [v.2]. This is the same work Luke has shown Jesus doing. Because that work depends only on God's power, it needs no special equipment or supplies [v.3]. In fact, as Jesus describes it in Luke's narration, it needs nothing but the willingness to go to a household and ask to stay there while one tells the Good News and brings healing to the whole town [v.4]. We hear Jesus say it's not a mission in which you need to worry about success. Should you find no welcome for your message, let those who've rejected it see that you're moving on unburdened by even a speck of failure [v.5]. Then, says Luke, the specially chosen twelve disciples (see 6:14–16) went out and fulfilled their mission [v.6].

Luke says Herod was puzzled by reports about Jesus' work—work that was now being shared by his disciples—because he couldn't figure out what sort of person would do such work [vv.7–9]. His fretting, as Luke describes it, suggests that Herod was still as anxious to control things around him as he'd been when he put John, now dead, in prison (see 3:20). In Luke's description, he doesn't seem at all interested in the forgiveness of God that was proclaimed by the prophets and was symbolized in the belief that Elijah would return to announce the fulfillment of God's plan (see Mal.3:23–24). Herod's desire to see Jesus is described as no more than an anxious curiosity.

THE TWELVE RETURNED FROM THEIR MISSION WITH MUCH STILL TO LEARN [LK.9:10–17]

[10] The apostles returned and told Jesus what they'd done. He went off with them privately toward the town of Bethsaida. [11] Many people learned this and followed. He welcomed them, told them of the kingdom of God and healed those in need of care. [12] At day's end, the twelve said, "Send the crowd away from this isolated place to the nearby farms or villages for food and shelter." [13] "You feed them," he said. They said, "We've only five loaves and two fish—unless we were to go buy provisions for everybody." [14] (The number of men alone was five thousand.) He told the disciples, "Have them sit in groups of about fifty." [15] They did as directed, and everyone settled. [16] He took the five loaves and two fish, looked to heaven, blessed them, divided them, and gave them to the disciples to give the

crowd. ¹⁷ They ate until they were full. When the leftovers were gathered, they filled twelve baskets.

Luke tells us Jesus headed to some quiet spot in the vicinity of Bethsaida, not far from where the Jordan flows into the Lake of Galilee—perhaps because he wanted time with the twelve to review their recent mission [v.10]. Although any hope of privacy was spoiled by crowds, we hear that Jesus reacted to their intrusion by speaking of God's kingdom—especially to those who needed its message of comfort and healing [v.11]. Luke describes the disciples as less patient than Jesus with the needs of the crowd [v.12], and we hear them reacting with incredulity to the command to feed them [v.13]. Luke asks us to picture a huge crowd and tells us Jesus' minimal instructions for preparing to eat [v.14].

After everyone was prepared [v.15], says Luke, Jesus held what was clearly an inadequate amount of food for thousands and focused on the need for much more. Where else would he look to satisfy such a need but to his Father in heaven? He then blessed the bread and fish—that is, he gave thanks for them as part of the blessings God was constantly providing—broke them into pieces, and asked the disciples to distribute them [v.16]. When Luke reports that the crowd not only ate well but couldn't finish all that was provided [v.17], we may wonder—as some of the disciples and others in the crowd may have wondered—how Jesus took care of this need with such apparent ease. If we try, as perhaps they did at the time, to figure it out, we're missing the point of the story. The point is at the heart of Luke's narration of the incident: Jesus looked to the Father.

JESUS EXPLAINS WHAT IT MEANS TO FOLLOW HIM
[LK.9:18–27]

¹⁸ Another time, alone with his disciples, Jesus had been praying. He asked them, "Who do the crowds say I am?" ¹⁹ "John the Baptist," they said. "Others say, Elijah." "Some say, 'a prophet of old has returned.'" 20 "And you," he asked, "who do you say I am?" Peter said, "God's Anointed." 21 Then he said very clearly: "Don't say this to others." 22 He told them, "The Son of Man will undergo much; will be rejected by chief priests and scribes, be killed and, on the third day, be raised. 23 To follow me, you must deny yourself, pick up your cross daily, and follow me. 24 To save your 'self' is to lose it. If you lose yourself for me, you'll save your life. 25 What's it worth to lose your 'self,' even if you get the whole world? 26 Are you put off by me and my words? Then the Son of Man will put you off when he comes in glory—the glory of the Father and all his angels. 27 I tell you the truth: some of those standing here won't taste death until they see the kingdom of God."

Above, Luke told us Jesus asked his disciples about their weak faith (8:25) and then gave them powerful evidence of his own faith (9:16). Here, Luke shows us that the disciples still don't understand the lessons of their teacher. Their responses to Jesus' question about people's opinions [v.18] seem almost perfunctory [v.19]. According to Luke, Jesus had to ask their opinion. They didn't offer it instinctively. When Peter says Jesus is God's anointed one, the Messiah [v.20], Luke says Jesus responded by telling them not to share this opinion [v.21].

Although Luke doesn't comment on this command, he does tell us Jesus immediately followed it with a description of what he saw ahead of him as someone who placed all trust in God. One wonders if the aspects of rejection and death in the description fit the disciples' picture of a Messiah.

Luke has already described Jewish teachers strongly rejecting Jesus' teaching (see 6:11; 7:30). Here he describes Jesus spelling out for the disciples how that rejection would eventually be complete—and fatal. But there's no need for the disciples to be horrified by this rejection, for Jesus assures them he'll be raised from death [v.22]. In fact, if they want to follow him into life after death, they'll have to follow him into the experience of carrying the burden, or cross, of personal failure [v.23]. This experience will overwhelm them if they try to grapple with it by themselves; but it will lead to salvation if they put the complete management of it in God's hands [v.24]. Luke describes Jesus saying that, if his followers seek deliverance from misery by amassing worldly comforts, they'll arrive at nothing [v.25]; and if they reject his way to glory, he will allow them to do so—and then they'll never find it [v.26]. But, if they choose to follow him and share his trust in God, they'll experience the kingdom of God before their deaths [v.27].

SOME DISCIPLES SEE JESUS GLORIFIED [LK.9:28–36]

[28] About eight days after this [talk of suffering, death, and being raised], Jesus took Peter, John, and James, and climbed a mountain to pray. [29] As he prayed, his face changed, and his clothes shimmered white. [30] Imagine, two men were talking with him—Moses and Elijah. [31] They appeared, glorified, and spoke of the exodus he would make in Jerusalem. [32] Peter and the others had been heavy with sleep, but they started awake to see the glory of Jesus and the two men with him. [33] As the two moved away, Peter said, "Master, it's good we're here. We can raise three tents—for you, for Moses, for Elijah." He didn't know what he was saying. [34] As he spoke, a cloud overshadowed them. They were fearful as they entered it. [35] From the cloud a voice said, "This is my Son, the one chosen. Listen to him." [36] When the voice had spoken, Jesus was seen alone. They said nothing—nor did they speak in those days of what they'd seen.

Luke's mention of praying reminds us that Jesus was constantly turning to the Father. In this instance, Jesus seems to want to be away from distraction and to instruct his closest disciples by his example [v.28]. Luke tells us that, in prayer, Jesus experienced the Father's glory. This was an experience of God's presence shared with Moses (who had accepted God's promise in the Covenant always to be present with his people) and with Elijah (who had called God's people to remember that promise). Luke depicts Jesus, Moses, and Elijah talking about the fulfillment of God's promise that would be completed when Jesus took leave of this life (his "exodus" from Jerusalem) to return to the Father [vv.29–31].

Luke depicts the disciples as comically untouched by the glory they witnessed. They'd been sleeping, not turning to God with Jesus, and when they woke and saw the effect of Jesus' prayer, Peter's sleepy response was to suggest putting this manifestation of God's glory into tents. Luke calls this muddled suggestion to memorialize the moment nonsense [vv.32–33] and says it was followed by a sign of God's presence that enveloped the disciples—presumably causing silence as it filled them with awe [v.34]. The voice of God, says Luke, echoed the delight expressed at the time of Jesus' baptism (see 3:22) and told the disciples to listen to his Son [v.35]—a task already given to them (see 8:18)—because Jesus, no one else, was the one God had chosen to bring his promises to fulfillment. Luke describes the disciples as dumbfounded by this experience. Apparently they could only wonder about the glory they'd experienced and the command they'd heard; they couldn't yet give witness to it.

EXAMPLES OF MISUNDERSTANDING JESUS [LK.9:37–50]

[37] *When they came down the mountain the next day, he was met by a large crowd.* [38] *A man in the crowd cried, "Teacher, I beg you to help my son, my only child.* [39] *A spirit makes him scream, convulse, foam at the mouth; then it leaves him crushed.* [40] *I begged your disciples to cast it out, but they couldn't."* [41] *"What a faithless, wrong-headed generation," said Jesus. "How long must I be with you and put up with you? Bring your son here."* [42] *As the boy approached, the demon knocked him down and convulsed him. Jesus gave the unclean spirit a command, healed the boy, and gave him back to his father.* [43] *While all marveled at God's mighty action and his works, he spoke to the disciples.* [44] *"Set these words in your ears: the Son of Man will be handed into men's hands."* [45] *They didn't understand this and couldn't puzzle it out, and were afraid to ask.* [46] *Then they began to argue which of them would be greatest.* [47] *Jesus saw what was on their minds. He brought a child to his side.* [48] *"Whoever receives this child in my name, receives me. And whoever receives me, receives the one who sent me. The least among you is the one who is great."* [49] *John said, "Master, when we saw*

someone casting out demons in your name, we tried to stop him because he didn't follow along with us." [50] *"Don't hinder him," said Jesus. "Whoever isn't against you is for you."*

———◆◇◆———

Luke tells us a crowd had gathered [v.37] around the waiting disciples who hadn't gone up the mountain (see 9:28). These disciples had been unable to help a needy father. Luke says Jesus couldn't understand why they hadn't put faith in God's power rather than their own. How often must he teach them to turn to God? Then, says Luke, Jesus taught the lesson of faith once again [vv.38–41]. Luke depicts the boy in the grip of his ailment, but shows Jesus trusting that the healing command he spoke was the will of God [v.42].

When Luke says Jesus turned from the admiring crowd to speak to the disciples about becoming a victim, he notes that the disciples didn't know what he meant and, like poor students, wouldn't reveal their ignorance [vv.44–45]. It seems they not only forgot what Jesus recently told them about the danger he faced (see 9:22), but also hadn't learned his most basic lesson: God is at work in all events. Hadn't they just seen God at work in a sick boy?

The disciples wouldn't ask Jesus about being "handed into men's hands," but they were eager to rank their achievements [v.46]—presumably as famous healers. Luke says Jesus realized the disciples needed another lesson. So he told them that, if they accepted his example of being childlike, they'd have to accept dependence on the Father. Whoever depends most on the Father's gifts is the one who is truly great—the one who needs (and gets) the most gifts [vv.47–48]. When John asked about healers who are outside their group, but nonetheless imitate Jesus' trust, Jesus said, "If they're seeking God's help and care, they're just like us."

IT'S TIME TO BE TAKEN COMPLETELY INTO THE FATHER'S CARE [LK.9:51–62]

[51] As the time came for him to be taken up, Jesus set his eyes toward Jerusalem. [52] He sent messengers ahead to a Samaritan city to prepare for a stop there. [53] But they wouldn't welcome him because he was headed to Jerusalem. [54] When James and John saw this they asked, "Lord, do you want us to call down fire from heaven to consume them—just as Elijah did [2 Kgs.1:10]?" [55] Jesus turned to them with a rebuke. [56] They went to another village. [57] On the way, someone said, "I'll follow wherever you go." [58] "Foxes have dens, birds have nests," said Jesus, "but the Son of Man has no place to rest his head." [59] He said to someone else, "Follow me," who replied, "Lord, let me first bury my father." [60] "Let the dead bury the dead," he said; "but you go proclaim the kingdom of God." [61] Another said, "I'll follow you, Lord, after I say farewell to my family." [62] Jesus said, "No one who puts a hand to the plow and looks back is fit for the kingdom of God."

————⟨ଉଉ⟩————

Luke has told us that, while Jesus' glory was being revealed to three of his disciples, Moses and Elijah conversed with him about his coming "exodus" (see 9:31). Here Luke points out that this will not be simply an exodus from earthly life, but a going into glory. In order to let himself be taken up completely into the glory of the Father, says Luke, Jesus heads to Jerusalem, the central place for Jews to give witness to what they believe [v.51]. Luke says Samaritans, who shared many Jewish beliefs but didn't accept the need to worship in Jerusalem, refused to welcome Jesus as a pilgrim on his way there [vv.52–53]. Some disciples are described reacting to this rejection as though they hadn't heard Jesus' instructions for dealing with resistance to the Good News about the kingdom (see 9:5). This, says Luke, provoked a correction from their teacher, who then set the proper example—by moving on [vv.54–56].

As he traveled, Luke tells us, Jesus continued to address the challenges facing those who want to follow him on his way to accepting God's glory. Taking that way doesn't require much—not even things we might consider essential, such as a home [vv.57–58]. Once you choose that way, you have no greater responsibility than to tell others about God's kingdom. Nothing is more important [vv.59–60]. Those who set off following Jesus to the kingdom will be distracted along that way. If, however, they follow their distractions rather than continuing on the way—well, perhaps God's kingdom wouldn't suit them [vv.61–62].

TEN

Traveling toward Jerusalem, Jesus Teaches about Discipleship

[1] The Lord sent seventy-two disciples, in pairs, to visit the towns where he planned to stop on his way to Jerusalem. [2] "The harvest is so plentiful," he said, "but there are so few laborers. Ask the Lord of the harvest to send out more workers into the harvest! [3] Go. You see, I send you like lambs among wolves. [4] Take no money bag, sack, or sandals. Don't fall in with people along the way. [5] When you enter a house, say, 'Peace to this house!' [6] If a child of peace lives there, the peace will have effect. If not, it will return to you. [7] Stay in one house. Don't move around. Eat what's offered—a worker should be paid. [8] Yes, eat what they set before you in a town that welcomes you. [9] Cure the sick there. Tell the inhabitants, 'The kingdom of God has come to you.' [10] If a town doesn't welcome you, make an announcement in their streets. [11] Shaking your feet, say, 'Keep even your dust! But know, God's kingdom is near.' [12] I say it will be more bearable for Sodom on the day of its coming than for that town."

—————◦◊◦—————

Here Luke depicts Jesus asking a large number of followers to share his sense of urgency about gathering people into the kingdom [vv.1–2]. Luke says Jesus gave these followers instructions similar to the guidance he first gave to the twelve (see 9:2–5)—instructions that indicate the task will seem daunting [v.3]. However, because they'll be proclaiming an invitation to share God's gifts, not selling merchandise, they'll need neither travel gear nor a network of new associates [v.4]. If a household wants to accept the gift of God's peace, it will; but disciples needn't worry about chilly receptions [vv.5–6]. They should take care not to create the impression that they're using the Good News to become honored guests in homes all around the towns they visit; but they can let someone in each town supply their room and board while they announce the healing news of the kingdom [vv.7–9].

We also hear that Jesus told the crowd of disciples that, even if people react negatively to their message, they should still tell that dismissive town about the closeness of God's kingdom. He gives them a short scene with dialogue to act out: "We won't trouble you further; and your rejection won't trouble us. Not even the dirt from this town will burden our feet as we continue our mission. Just one last word: God's kingdom is coming" [vv.10–11]. Then, says Luke, Jesus mentioned the people of Sodom—people who never heard about God's kingdom—and compared them to those who do hear about the kingdom. His assertion implies the question: "Who will be more remorseful on the Day of Judgment, when the kingdom is revealed in all its glory: those who heard about the kingdom and rejected it, or those who are hearing about it for the first time?" [v.12].

HOW WOEFUL TO REJECT GOD'S WORD; HOW SATISFYING TO TAKE IT IN [LK.10:13–24]

[13] *Jesus continued to speak to the disciples he was sending out: "Woe to you, Chorazin; woe to you, Bethsaida. If the mighty works done in you had been done in Tyre and Sidon, they'd long ago have repented in sackcloth and ashes.* [14] *Tyre and Sidon will bear up on the Day of Judgment better than you.* [15] *And you, Capernaum, [recall Isaiah:] 'Lifted to heaven? No, cast into Hades!'* [16] *Whoever*

listens to you, my disciples, listens to me. Whoever rejects you rejects me and the one who sent me." [17] The seventy-two came back rejoicing: "Lord, in your name, even demons obey us." [18] He said, "I saw Satan fall from the sky like lightning. [19] Look, I've given you ability to tread on snakes and scorpions—authority over the power of the enemy. Nothing can harm you. [20] Don't exult that spirits obey you but that your names are written in heaven." [21] Reveling in the Holy Spirit, he said, "I praise you, Father, Lord of heaven and earth, because of what you hid from the wise and knowing but, ah, were glad to show to babes. [22] My Father entrusted all things to me. No one knows the Son but the Father. And no one knows the Father except the Son—and anyone to whom the Son reveals him." [23] To the disciples alone, Jesus said, "Happy are the eyes that see what you see. [24] I tell you, many prophets and kings wanted to see what you see, but didn't see; to hear what you hear, but didn't hear."

———❦———

Though Luke doesn't say whether Jesus addressed the first words here to the seventy-two (see 10:1) or to other followers, he clearly makes the point that Jesus added more warnings about rejecting the call to repentance (see 10:10–12). Jewish towns that rejected Jesus' witness to God's power—thinking, perhaps, they could achieve power for themselves (see Is.14:13–15)—would be judged by that rejection. Gentile communities such as Tyre or Sidon, which neither knew the scriptures nor heard Jesus teaching, would be judged differently [vv.13–16].

Luke tells us that, when the seventy-two returned with beginners' enthusiasm [v.17], Jesus shared their delight in seeing evil thrown down and in trusting that no hurt comes to those who trust in God [vv.18–19]. But he also reminded them their power was not their own. It came from the Father who kept their names before him always [v.20]. This image of God so touched Jesus, says Luke, that he was inspired to thank God for filling the helpless with notions of divine goodness (see 6:20) while letting pedants get lost in their thoughts [v.21]. We hear Jesus saying that coming to know God is a gift, and that others must be instructed about that gift [v.22]. Luke says Jesus told his disciples they were lucky to be sharing this instruction with him. Famous prophets and kings had wanted to savor the kind of spiritual conversation Jesus and his disciples were enjoying. But they had found no one with whom to share their desire [vv.23–24].

LEARNING FROM JESUS [LK.10:25–42]

[25] Once, a lawyer tested Jesus, asking, "Teacher, what will bring me eternal life?" [26] Jesus said, "What's written in the Law? How do you read it?" [27] He said, "You should love the Lord your God with all your heart, your soul, your might, your mind, and love your neighbor as yourself." [28] "Right," said Jesus. "Do this, and live." [29] Hoping to defend his question, the lawyer asked, "But, who's my 'neighbor'?" [30] Jesus said, "A man going from Jerusalem to Jericho met bandits who stripped and beat him, leaving him half dead. [31] A priest passed along the road, saw him, and kept to the other side. [32] A Levite came along the same road, saw him, and kept to the other side. [33] But a Samaritan came along, saw him, and was moved with pity. [34] He dressed his wounds, took him to a caravansary on his beast, and cared for him. [35] The next day he gave two silver coins to the manager of the caravansary and said, 'Take care of him. If you spend more, I'll pay on my return.' [36] Which of the three seems to you to be a neighbor to the bandits' victim?" [37] "The one who was kind to him," he said. "Go do the same," said Jesus. [38] On their trip they entered a town where a woman named Martha welcomed him. [39] Her sister, Mary, sat at the Lord's feet listening to him. [40] But Martha, worried about serving a meal, said, "Lord, don't you see my sister's left me alone with the serving? Tell her to help me." [41] "Martha, Martha," said the Lord, "you worry about too much. [42] One thing's required. Mary wanted that one thing. It won't be taken from her."

—◦◦◦—

Luke tells us that along the way to Jerusalem Jesus was challenged by a Jewish legal expert to explain how one reached the kingdom—that is, eternal life [v.25]. The man, says Luke, knew the Law [v.26] and could cite passages (see Dt.6:5; Lv.19:18) that answered his own question [vv.27–28]. Then Luke says Jesus defined "neighbor" by telling a story that led to the question, "What's the difference between those who ignore another's suffering, and a person who's moved by it?" After the lawyer admitted that the Samaritan acted as a neighbor to a stranger in need, we hear Jesus do more than agree. He asked the lawyer to let himself be moved by compassion for others [vv.29–37]—just as we've seen Jesus doing (see, e.g., 7:13).

Luke then offers a different example of learning from Jesus. After describing Martha as an attentive friend—or neighbor—he says Jesus corrected her assumption that there's only one way to attend to another's needs. In fact, if you're looking for the one thing that's necessary in life, you should seek to listen to Jesus' teaching. Nothing should get in the way of that [vv.38–42]. Unless we learn Jesus' lesson about allowing oneself to be moved by the needs around us as God is moved by them, we'll only respond to someone else's needs as Martha, the priest, and the Levite responded—with our individual impulse.

ELEVEN

What to Expect from God, Your Father

WHAT IS PRAYER? [LK.11:1–13]

¹ Once, along the way to Jerusalem, Jesus was praying. After he finished, a disciple said, "Lord, teach us to pray as John taught his disciples." ² "When you pray," he said, "say, 'Father, make your name glorified; make your kingdom come. ³ Each day, give us our daily bread. ⁴ Forgive our faults, for we forgive faults against us. Spare our faith the ultimate test.' ⁵ Now, suppose someone goes to a friend at midnight saying, 'Lend me some bread. ⁶ A friend has traveled to see me, but I have nothing to give him.' ⁷ But the friend says, 'Go away; the door's locked. The children are asleep. I can't get it now.' ⁸ And yet, if friendship won't get that man up, pestering will rouse him to give what's needed. ⁹ I say: ask, and it'll be given; seek, and you'll find; knock, the door will be opened. ¹⁰ It's askers who receive, seekers who find; and those who knock get the door opened. ¹¹ If you're a parent, and your child asks for a fish, will you give a snake? ¹² If asked for an egg, will you give a scorpion? ¹³ If you selfish ones know how to give good things to your children, how much more will the Father in heaven give the Holy Spirit to those who ask him?"

⎯⎯ᎧᎧ⎯⎯

When Luke tells us here that the disciples asked to learn the sort of praying taught by the Baptist, he's letting us know that they hadn't yet learned to pray from Jesus' example (see, e.g., 9:16; 10:21). So he describes Jesus putting into simple petitions some basic lessons he'd been teaching them—and had also been using. He said: ask the Father to turn all hearts to himself (see 4:8); ask him to gather all souls into his kingdom [v.2]; let the Father take care of you (v.3; see 4:4); notice your failures to forgive (see 6:37), and ask to be forgiven for those failures. Also ask your Father to shield your weak trust in him from an ultimate test [v.4]. Luke's depiction of this lesson in prayer stresses the fact that every moment in a disciple's unfolding relationship with the Father—from first turning to receive God's glory to becoming completely confident in his care—needs, and will receive, God's helpful attention.

Luke says Jesus asked his disciples to notice how sensible it was to appeal to the Father for their deepest needs. Don't they lean on their friends when they're desperate [vv.5–8]? Certainly they know that only by pursuing what they seek or need can they hope to find it [vv.9–10]. Do they suppose that, if they ran to God, God would be less attentive and generous than they are [vv.11–12]? "Admit it," we hear Jesus say. "You're all distracted by selfishness, even when you deal with your children. Nonetheless, you manage to care for them. Well, your Father isn't distracted by selfishness, and he wants to give you the same divine Spirit he's given to me (see 3:22; 4:14; 10:21). What would keep him from giving it to you [v.13]?"

WHAT IS EVIL? [LK.11:14–26]

[14] *[Still on the way to Jerusalem,] Jesus cast out a demon who'd made a man mute. The crowds were startled that the man spoke.* [15] *Some said, "He casts out demons by Beelzebul, the prince of demons."* [16] *Some others, wanting evidence, asked him for a sign from heaven.* [17] *He knew how they thought. "Every kingdom divided against itself is ruined, with one house falling on another.* [18] *If Satan divides against himself, how can his kingdom stand? How can you say I cast out demons by Beelzebul?* [19] *I cast out by Beelzebul? By whom do your exorcists cast*

them out? They're your gauge. ²⁰ Now, if I expel demons by God's finger, then God's kingdom has come. ²¹ When a strong, heavily armed man guards his house, his goods are safe. ²² If someone stronger overcomes him, he takes the trusted arms and all else. ²³ Anyone not with me is against me. Anyone who doesn't gather with me scatters. ²⁴ When a polluting spirit comes out of someone, it roams the wastes seeking rest. Finding none, it says, 'I'll go back where I came from.' ²⁵ But it finds the place swept—all in order. ²⁶ It returns with seven spirits more evil than itself. When they settle in, that fate's worse than the first."

Here Luke describes Jesus again facing skepticism. Like the people of Nazareth (see 4:22), people in this crowd tried to explain away what they'd witnessed—in this case, Jesus' power over the realm of Beelzebul, the one who claims to control worldly power (see 4:6–7; vv.14–16). Luke tells us Jesus confronted the crowd with the ridiculous picture of Satan's kingdom warring with itself. Then he asked them to consider how nonsensical it would be for any exorcist to appeal to Beelzebul to cast out of people the demons he's supposedly insinuated into people [vv.17–19].

Next, says Luke, Jesus asked the crowd to consider several things: first, the possibility that God was at work in him and was having an effect in their lives [v.20]; second, if God's power is stronger than the forces of this world, God can overcome those forces [vv.21–22]; and, third, if Jesus' teaching is true—if God's power is at work in us—then chasing after worldly power would be like trying to run, or scatter, in all directions at once [v.23].

As Luke tells it, Jesus concluded his address to this crowd by illustrating the power of bedevilment with a description of a home-invading demon determined to return to its familiar abode [v.24]. When it received no welcome from the person who'd been healed of it [v.25], it got help from other selfish forces and afflicted the healed person with greater distress [v.26]. (To whom could such a distressed person turn for deliverance from such evil?)

WHAT IS HAPPINESS? [LK.11:27–36]

[27] A woman in the crowd that Jesus was addressing cried, "Happy the womb that bore you, the breasts at which you nursed." [28] "No," he said, "happy are they who hear God's word and cherish it." [29] As more people crowded around, he said, "This is an evil generation seeking a sign. It will get no sign but the sign of Jonah. [30] Jonah was a sign to the Ninevites just as the Son of Man will be to this generation. [31] The queen of the south will be raised at Judgment with this generation and condemn it. She traveled far to hear Solomon's wisdom, and look, greater than Solomon is here. [32] The Ninevites will stand with this generation at Judgment and condemn it. They repented when they heard Jonah's preaching. And look, greater than Jonah is here. [33] No one lights a lamp to hide it or cover it; you put it on a stand so others can see. [34] The body's lamp is the eye. When the eye is healthy, the whole body's affected by light. If it's unhealthy, the body's in the dark. [35] Watch out that you're not filled with darkness. [36] If the body is all light—if it has no darkness—it will give light just as a lamp does."

———⟨∞⟩———

According to Luke, Jesus not only corrected a mistaken notion of bliss by pointing out that the word of God was the sole source of happiness [vv.27–28] but also chastised his hearers for seeking an assurance that God would keep his word to care for them [v.29a]. Had they never read the Book of Jonah [v.29b]? That story should have made them ashamed. The people of Nineveh repented and turned to God as soon as they heard from Jonah that believing in God was better than trusting in themselves. But this age was rejecting that same message when it was repeated to them by Jesus [vv.30, 32]. The story of the Queen of Sheba (see 1 Kgs.10:1–10) should also have shamed them. That powerful foreign woman was willing to believe in the promises of the God of Israel. But this generation wasn't listening to Jesus teach the same truth [v.31].

What Jesus claimed to be doing, says Luke, was as simple as putting a lamp on a table (cf. 8:16). He was giving light [v.33]. Light allows those with good eyes to move about freely and confidently, said Jesus, but those with eye problems get less help from light [v.34]. Luke portrays Jesus thinking this image is easy to understand: "Seek and savor my word just as you eagerly look for light when it's dark [v.35]. The more you fill yourself with my instruction, the more will my lessons be clear and comforting to you — just as one feels happily at home in a well-lit room" [v.36].

WHAT IS SELFISHNESS? [LK.11:37–54]

37 *After Jesus finished speaking to that crowd [see 11:14], a Pharisee invited him to dinner. He went and reclined at table.* 38 *The Pharisee was shocked to see he didn't wash before he ate.* 39 *The Lord said to him, "You Pharisees clean the surface of a cup or plate, but inside you're caked with greed and wickedness.* 40 *Fools. Didn't he who made the outside make the inside too?* 41 *Give alms for what's inside. Imagine: you'll be all clean!* 42 *Alas, you Pharisees tithe mint, rue, and other herbs but ignore God's way of judging and loving. Do both!* 43 *Alas, you Pharisees love high seats in the synagogue and deference at the markets.* 44 *Woe to you. You're like unmarked graves over which others walk unaware."* 45 *A lawyer spoke up: "Teacher, these words are also insulting to us."* 46 *"Woe also to you lawyers," he said. "You put burdens on others, but lend no hand.* 47 *Alas, you build memorials for the very prophets your ancestors killed.* 48 *Your witness to their murderous deeds is to build memorials to them.* 49 *God's wisdom said: 'I'll send them prophets and emissaries to persecute and kill.'* 50 *This age must answer for all prophets' blood spilled from the world's beginning.* 51 *Yes, you'll have to answer for blood from Abel to Zechariah—killed near the altar [2 Chr.24:22]!* 52 *Alas, you lawyers, you took wisdom's key, didn't use it, and locked others out."* 53 *Jesus left the house, leaving the Pharisees and scribes feeling deeply resentful—and anxious to interrogate him meticulously.* 54 *They wanted to trap him with one of his own pronouncements.*

—⚬⚬⚬—

Luke tells us Jesus noted that Pharisees (defenders of the Law) were so obsessed with proper appearances that they were blind to their improper desires [vv.37–40]. And yet, if they concerned themselves with the needs of others and gave alms, they might become aware of—and cleansed from—their selfish desires [v.41]. Luke says Jesus saw the Pharisees spending their energy on details of the Law such as tithing (offering 10 percent of all goods) without remembering the essential purpose of the Law (see Dt.6:5). Signs of respect, says Jesus, play out as farces when the object of reverence is rotten within [vv.42–44].

According to Luke, a complaint [v.45] provoked Jesus to point out that lawyers (scholars of the Mosaic Law, or "scribes") perverted the Law with as much ignorant gusto as the Pharisees: they told others what the Law imposed but didn't fulfill its obligations [v.46]; they saw themselves as defenders of the Law, but didn't see how, like their ancestors, they rejected the prophets' call to repentance [vv.47–48]. Yes, says Jesus, to spurn God's word is to participate in slaughtering all his messengers, and in hiding the message from others [vv.49–52].

This strong lesson stirred the diners to resentment and anger, not to reflection or repentance [vv.53–54].

TWELVE

Making a Choice between the Spirit of God and the Spirit of the Times

GOD'S SPIRIT INSPIRES CANDOR AND CALM [LK.12:1–12]

¹ Once, there was a crowd so large that people trampled one another. Jesus began to speak just to his disciples: "Beware the leaven—the hypocrisy—of the Pharisees. ² Nothing's hidden that won't be revealed; there's no secret that won't be known. ³ What you say in the dark will be heard in the light; what's murmured indoors will be proclaimed from the roof. ⁴ Listen, my friends, don't be afraid of those who kill the body, and can do no more. ⁵ I'll show you whom to fear: the one who can kill the body then drag it to Gehenna. ⁶ Five sparrows go for two copper coins. But not one of them is unknown to God. ⁷ Even the hairs on your head are counted. So, fear not. You're worth more than birds. ⁸ I tell you, if you speak out for me before others, I'll own you before God's angels. ⁹ And if you reject me before others, I'll disown you in front of God's angels. ¹⁰ Whoever speaks against the Son of Man will be forgiven. But whoever speaks against the Holy Spirit will not be forgiven. ¹¹ Now, if they bring you before synagogues, rulers, or other authorities, don't fret about what to say in your defense. ¹² At that hour, the Holy Spirit will teach you what to say."

—⌁⌁⌁—

Luke describes Jesus surrounded by mayhem, yet speaking as if one needn't react anxiously to a mob scene. Specifically, we hear Jesus warning the disciples not to react to any situation as the Pharisees do (see above) by cloaking everything in sanctimony [v.1]. No amount of flummery can conceal our anxieties, says Jesus. It's better to admit them, because we can't keep them secret [vv.2–3]. It's not a mystery that someone stronger than you can kill you [v.4]. And it's not a mystery that wicked urges, personified by the devil, can lead you to endless torment, like the perpetually smoldering fire called Gehenna [v.5]. But, says Jesus, there's no need to fear such threats, for God's care covers every detail of life—even small birds and balding heads [vv.6–7].

Then, says Luke, Jesus spelled out what this lesson implied: if the Good News is true—if there's nothing to fear—then all who accept that news will share it, and Jesus will express his delight before God at this impulse to share his message [v.8]. On the other hand, those who reject the news will be recognized for their rejection [v.9]. Luke tells us Jesus made clear he wasn't seeking personal approval. Anyone who argued with him could be forgiven for doing so—leaving the possibility of repentance for later. But those who simply refused to imagine God might be working hard to give us his own Spirit were rejecting all possibility of reconciliation and forgiveness [v.10]. When the disciples encounter this sort of rejection directed at them, they needn't fear—unless, of course, they don't trust God's Spirit to inspire them [vv.11–12].

THIS WORLD INSPIRES WORRY [LK.12:13–32]

[13] *Someone in the unruly crowd [see 12:1] said, "Teacher, tell my brother to share our inheritance."* [14] *"Sir," he said, "who made me your executor or judge?"* [15] *He said to all, "Guard against greed. Luxury doesn't make a rich life."* [16] *He told a parable: "A rich man's farm produced a superabundant crop.* [17] *The man wondered, 'Where will I store all this produce?* [18] *I know,' he said; 'I'll tear down these barns and build larger ones for all my goods.* [19] *I can brag to myself: "You've got enough for years, so eat, drink and be merry."'* [20] *But God said, 'Fool.*

Tonight I call in your life. Whose are your goods now?' [21] *It's the same for anyone storing up things, but not enriched by God."* [22] *To his disciples Jesus said, "Don't worry about life—what to eat, what to wear.* [23] *Life's more than food; and the body's more than clothing.* [24] *Look at ravens. They don't sow, reap, or have barns. God feeds them. You're more important than birds.* [25] *Can worry bring you one more moment of life?* [26] *If you can't do that little thing, why worry about anything else?* [27] *Watch lilies bloom. They don't work or spin, but Solomon never looked so good.* [28] *If God dresses up plants that flourish one day and are burnt the next, won't he dress you? So little faith.* [29] *Don't fret about eating or drinking. Let go of that anxiety.* [30] *That's what the world frets about. Your Father knows you need those things.* [31] *Hanker instead for the kingdom of heaven. All the rest is given besides.* [32] *Don't fret, little flock. The Father delights in giving you the kingdom.*

Here Luke shows us Jesus declining to rescue someone whose distress is caused not by need but by a bruised sense of entitlement [vv.13–15]. Then the parable narrated by Luke highlights the foolishness of thinking we can plan full, happy lives for ourselves. It stresses the obvious flaw in such a plan: our basic ignorance. How ridiculous we look when we try to shape lives whose dimensions are being set by God, not by us [vv.16–21].

Luke says Jesus told his disciples not to worry how God cares for basic needs [v.22]. There are even deeper needs [v.23]. The world is full of rich and abundant forms of life that the disciples can't begin to replicate. Life keeps unfolding, but the disciples can't add a moment to it. How foolish to put faith in oneself rather than the one who creates life [vv.24–28].

We hear the disciples being told not to imitate those who are so obsessed with their appetites that they never think of the God who made their appetites. God knows not only what they need today, but also what they will need always: his kingdom [vv.29–31]. Luke describes Jesus calling his disciples a little flock—sheep who need pasture and protection. Do they think the Father doesn't know that?

He wants to give them more than food. He wants to give them himself [v.32].

HOW TO CHOOSE GOD'S SPIRIT [LK.12:33–48]

33 Jesus told his disciples, "Sell what you have and give away the proceeds. Keep your wealth in heaven, where no thief goes and no moth munches. 34 Where your wealth is, there's your heart. 35 And keep your belts tight and your lamps lit. 36 Be like those waiting for a master's return from a wedding. Open at the first knock. 37 Happy those found watching! Yes indeed, I say the master will sit them at table, and serve them! 38 How happy they'll be if he arrives at midnight or dawn and still finds them waiting. 39 You know a man would bar a thief from his house if he knew his arrival time. 40 So, prepare yourselves for the Son of Man to come at an unexpected hour." 41 Peter asked, "Lord, do you tell this parable for us, or for all here?" 42 Jesus said, "Which wise, trusty servant does a master ask to feed and pay the others properly? 43 How happy will that servant be when the master shows up and finds him at his job. 44 Yes, I say he'll make him manager of everything he owns. 45 What if a servant, thinking, 'My master's late,' beats the others, and gets drunk? 46 The master will show up unexpectedly and cut him in two—a fate fit for the faithless. 47 A servant who knows a master's wishes and simply neglects them will be thrashed. 48 An ignorant slave who needs discipline will only get cuffed. Much is expected from those who get much, and much more from those who receive much more."

Just above, Luke describes Jesus telling his disciples to drop worldly worries. Here, he tells us what Jesus suggested they pick up instead: they should exchange worldly concerns for heavenly ones—that is, decide where their interests lie [vv.33–34]. Luke says Jesus told them if they chose heavenly riches they'd have to learn how to wait for them. They'd have to be perpetually ready [v.35], the way servants wait for the return of the head of the house. A master would be so delighted by a prepared household staff that he'd throw them a party—even if it's well past bedtime [vv.36–38]. Then, says Luke, Jesus put it another way. People who know the time of an important arrival at home prepare for it. Disciples should know that Jesus will ask how they are fulfilling their commission (see 10:9). They should always be ready to answer that question [vv.39–40].

Luke tells us Jesus answered Peter's question about the intended audience of the parable [v.41] by describing a good relationship between any master and servant: a good servant, or disciple, will take seriously the master's invitation to accept responsibilities. Such servants are likely to become close partners with their masters [vv.42–44]. But servants who use a master's house without regard for his wishes—well, what's likely to happen to them? Luke reports that Jesus thought there were many ways to ignore or misunderstand his teachings [vv.45–48a]. But the disciples who received the teaching gladly would be expected to deepen their pleasure in it [v.48b].

NOT EVERYONE WILL WANT GOD'S SPIRIT [LK.12:49–59]

[49] *Jesus continued, "I came to cast fire on the earth. I wish it were already blazing.* [50] *I am to be drenched in baptism; and my longing for it consumes me.* [51] *Do you think I came to bring peace on earth? No, I say instead, conflict.* [52] *Now there'll be conflict in a house of five, with two against three, three against two.* [53] *Father will conflict with son, son with father, mother with daughter, daughter with mother, mother-in-law with daughter-in-law, daughter-in-law with mother-in-law."* [54] *He turned from his disciples to the crowd: "When you see a cloud in the west, you say, 'It's going to rain.' And it does.* [55] *When the south wind blows, you say, 'It's going to be hot.' And it gets hot.* [56] *Fakers! You diagnose the look of the earth and sky, but won't assess this moment!* [57] *Why can't you tell what's right—what's important?* [58] *On the way to court with an accuser, find accord or he'll take you to the judge. The judge will hand you to the bailiff, and the bailiff will take you to prison.* [59] *I tell you, you won't escape until you pay the last small coin of your penalty."*

―――∽∾∽――――

Luke depicts Jesus suddenly speaking with great passion to his disciples, saying he wants to fire them up with the same dedication to God (see 3:21–22; 11:28) that consumes him [vv.49–50]. We hear it was Jesus' intention that his passion should unsettle them [v.51]—that is, confront them with the hard choice of either accepting and proclaiming his message about God's care (see 11:36; 12:8), or refusing it (see 12:8). Luke tells us Jesus was aware that choosing the first would lead to antagonism from anyone (including those in one's own house) who chose the latter [v.52]. According to Luke, Jesus said the divisions, dissensions, and debates caused by his word could rile any relationship—a picture of total family turbulence that seems grimly comic [v.53].

Then, says Luke, Jesus turned to give this message to the packed crowd (see 12:1). First, he made fun of their readiness to track every shift in the weather while they paid no attention to signs that told them something more important was happening in their midst [vv.54–55]. He had warned them against adopting the smug self-satisfaction of the Pharisees (see 12:1). Now he asks them to make the right choice—that is, to grapple with his message rather than to remain complacent, like the Pharisees [v.56]. Luke says Jesus used the image of an impending lawsuit to stress the importance of making this right choice. Those who assumed they were always right and had no impulse to listen to another point of view would be shocked when the ideas they so easily dismissed came under an objective review. The results of that review would cost them dearly [vv.58–59].

THIRTEEN

Now Is the Time for Repentance

WHAT IS SIN? HOW PATIENT IS GOD WITH SIN? [LK.13:1–9]

¹ [As he traveled toward Jerusalem,] Jesus was asked about some Galileans whose blood Pilate had mixed with sacrifices. ² Jesus said, "Do you think that happened because they were worse sinners than others? ³ I say, no. But, if you don't repent, you'll all meet a similar fate. ⁴ What about the eighteen crushed and killed by the tower that fell in Siloam? Were they more arrogant than all other inhabitants of Jerusalem? ⁵ I say, no. But, if you don't repent, you'll all perish that way." ⁶ Then he told a parable: "Once, a farmer had a fig tree that gave no fruit. ⁷ He told a gardener, 'I've looked for fruit on this tree for three years and found none. Cut it down. Why should it deplete the soil?' ⁸ 'My lord,' said the gardener, 'give it another year. I'll turn the soil and fertilize it. ⁹ It may yet bear fruit. If not, then cut it down.'"

———◦◦◦———

Luke depicts yet another encounter during Jesus' travels toward Jerusalem (see 9:51). Although he doesn't say precisely how Pilate desecrated the Galileans' blood, he lets us know the atrocity provoked people to ask Jesus, "What did they do to deserve such a fate?" Luke says Jesus first asked whether they thought the Galileans' end indicated an extraordinary degree of sinfulness or estrangement from God [vv.1–2]. Then he told them, in effect, they were making sin too mysterious. Sin is simply refusing to turn to God — refusing to repent of self-centeredness. Anyone who chooses not to repent is choosing desecration — choosing to be separated from God [v.3]. Luke tells us Jesus repeated this point by asking his listeners what they thought about a recent accident that may also have provoked the question of what they did to deserve it [v.4]. Was his audience horrified by that death blow? Well, he said, that's the sort of horror they should feel when they realize that they're unrepentant sinners [v.5].

Then, says Luke, Jesus told a story about a farmer who, while trying to decide how long he should wait for a seemingly useless tree to bear fruit, is easily persuaded to have more patience rather than less [vv.6–9]. The story provokes the question: how do we picture God — as a cost-conscious businessman, or as a person ready to hope for the best?

WHOSE DEEDS SHOULD WE ADMIRE, OURS OR GOD'S?
[LK.13:10–21]

[10] [On his way to Jerusalem,] Jesus taught in a town's synagogue one Sabbath. [11] A woman there, beset with a dispiriting illness for years, couldn't stand straight. [12] Jesus saw her and said, "Woman, you're free of your illness." [13] He placed his hands on her and she instantly straightened up, giving glory to God. [14] The synagogue leader was furious that Jesus had healed. He announced, "There are six work days. Come on one of those days to be cured, not on the Sabbath." [15] The Lord said, "Hypocrites! On the Sabbath, doesn't each of you untie ox and ass to take them to water? [16] Shouldn't this daughter of Abraham, knotted up by Satan, be untied on a Sabbath?" [17] Those opposed to him were abashed, but the whole crowd enjoyed his great deeds. [18] He asked, "What is God's kingdom like? To what shall I compare it? [19] It's like a planted mustard seed that grew into a tree where birds of the air could nest. [20] Yes, what shall I compare God's kingdom to? [21] It's like leavening a woman put into a large amount of flour, fermenting it all."

—⊂ᑲᑲᑲᕼ—

Luke's been describing Jesus' trek to Jerusalem as a trip filled with moments of instruction about accepting God's presence in our lives (see 9:51; 10:1). Here, he again depicts Jesus revealing God at work by responding to someone's need for healing—a response that occurred on a Sabbath [vv.10–11]. The woman who was healed is described as giving thanks to God that Jesus' concern led to the gift of well-being [vv.12–13]. But the overseer of Sabbath worship is described as castigating the whole assembly for countenancing any kind of work on the Sabbath [v.14]. Perhaps Luke imagined some worshipers looking chastened by this scolding, for he describes Jesus asking if they've ever let their livestock out of their stalls on a Sabbath and, if so, whether they thought a Sabbath was a proper day for a child of God to be freed from the bedeviling effects of sickness [vv.15–16]. Luke says some people were annoyed by the insinuation that blindly following the rules was mere sanctimony, while most people in the crowd were delighted to see Jesus' act of healing [v.17].

Then Luke describes Jesus asking his audience what they imagined when they pictured God at work fulfilling his promise to bring them to his kingdom. Did they envision God working in their lives as an unremarkable presence revealing itself slowly and unnoticed until its effect is eventually seen to be enormous and is felt everywhere? For those who may not have made that assumption, we hear Jesus offer two images to help them imagine that God, whom they do not see, might nonetheless be hard at work bringing his kingdom to fulfillment [vv.18–21].

THERE'S ONLY ONE WAY TO ENTER GOD'S KINGDOM
[LK.13:22–35]

²² He passed through many towns, teaching as he went. ²³ Someone asked, "Lord, are only a few to be saved?" He said: ²⁴ "Aim to enter through the narrow gate. Many will want to enter but won't be able. ²⁵ After the master of the house shuts the door, and you're standing outside clamoring, 'Open up, Lord,' the answer will be, 'I don't know you.' [26] *You'll say, 'We ate and drank with you; you taught in our streets.'* [27] *He'll say, 'I don't know where you're from: "Off, all who do evil!" [see Ps.6:9].'* [28] *There'll be tears and lamenting when you see Abraham, Isaac, Jacob, and the prophets in the kingdom of God and see yourselves outside.* [29] *People will come from east, west, north, and south to dine in God's kingdom.* [30] *Imagine, some who are last will be first, and some who are first will be last."* [31] *Then some Pharisees warned him, "Leave here. Herod wants to kill you."* [32] *He said, "You can tell that fox, 'Look, today and tomorrow I cast out demons and heal. On the third day, I finish.'* [33] *But today, tomorrow, and the next, I travel. A prophet can't die outside Jerusalem!* [34] *Jerusalem, Jerusalem, you kill prophets and stone messengers. How often I wanted to gather your children as a hen gathers chicks under her wing. You resisted me.* [35] *Your house is in ruins. You won't see me until you say, 'Blessed is the one who comes in the name of the Lord' [Ps.118:26]."*

———◦◦◦———

The person Luke depicts asking about salvation [vv.22–23] may have been touched by scripture's stories about faithlessness, or moved by Jesus' calls to repentance (see 13:3, 5). Jesus' reported answer about the "narrow gate" [v.24] may seem enigmatic, but Luke has consistently described him saying the only way to salvation is through the God who wants to give us freedom from all hurt. However, says Jesus, those who choose not to enter into this Covenant with God will be recognized for their choice [v.25]. Should they panic when a time of judgment comes and, like the people of Nazareth (see 4:22), claim to know him [v.26], Jesus will pray the Psalms, asking for protection from false friends [v.27]. O, how painful it will be when many of God's children realize that others love their Father more than they do [vv.28–30].

When Luke says Jesus mentioned a "third day" to the Pharisees [v.31], we may think of Jesus' three days in the tomb [v.32]. However, the image need not refer to the resurrection. It may simply make the point that Jesus intended to complete his itinerary [v.33a]. Then, says Luke, Jesus blurted out that he was going to Jerusalem because it was there that the call to repentance had been violently rejected —

yes, there, where the Lord's Temple stood as a constant reminder of the need for repentance [vv.33b–34a]. Luke portrays Jesus as distressed by his failure to call God's children back to the comfort of their abandoned nest, but also hopeful that they might yet see him as a teacher who was reminding them of that call [vv.34b–35].

FOURTEEN

Jesus Presses His Hearers to Make a Choice

JESUS ASKS RELIGIOUS PROFESSIONALS TO CONSIDER WHAT THEY WANT [LK.14:1–14]

[1] *Jesus dined with an eminent Pharisee on a Sabbath. They watched him closely.* [2] *Someone was present who suffered from painful swelling of the limbs.* [3] *Jesus asked the legal scholars and Pharisees, "May one cure on the Sabbath or not?"* [4] *They stayed silent. Jesus embraced the man, healed him, and sent him off.* [5] *He said, "If your child, or even your ox, fell into a trough on a Sabbath, wouldn't you pull him right out?"* [6] *They couldn't answer that either.* [7] *He then told a parable to the guests whom he saw angling for prominent places.* [8] *"When invited to a feast, don't take a high place. A greater guest may arrive.* [9] *Your host will say, 'Let this person have your place.' Chagrined, you slink lower.* [10] *When invited, take a low place. Then your host can say, 'Friend, come up here'—to the admiration of all the other guests.* [11] *Exalt yourself, and you'll be humbled. Humble yourself, you'll be exalted."* [12] *He said to his host, "Don't invite friends, relatives, or rich neighbors to dine. All you'll get is invitations in return.* [13] *Invite the poor, the paralyzed, the hobbled, and the blind.* [14] *How delightful that they can't repay you. You'll be repaid when the righteous rise."*

✦✦✦

Luke has told us that defenders and scholars of the Law (Pharisees and scribes) wanted to accuse Jesus of false teaching (see 11:54), and that at least one synagogue leader had reproved him for healing on a Sabbath (see 13:14). Here Luke describes Jesus challenging such religious leaders to say what they thought the Sabbath law allowed [v.3]; then depicts Jesus demonstrating his own opinion by freeing someone from physical suffering [v.4]. Jesus, says Luke, pushed this audience of respected experts to admit that the needs of a child (or even an animal) who was dear to them would prompt them to act with solicitude rather than self-righteousness. He was met by stony faces [vv.5–6].

According to Luke, Jesus kept trying to help this tough audience realize that thinking much of yourself was neither attractive nor realistic. They'd just been asked to imagine the outcome of cherishing a legal opinion more than a child. Now we hear Jesus ask them what it would be like if they went to a banquet assuming that everyone held them in the highest esteem, but arrived to find the assumption was wrong. How embarrassing [vv.7–9]! But how pleasant it would be to discover that your host thought more of you than you did of yourself [vv.10–11].

Won't it be a joy, says Jesus, to find at the time of your resurrection that, whenever you saw yourself among the feeble and lowly [v.13], God saw you as someone to whom he wanted to give his kingdom [v.14]. Compare that gift to a pile of invitations to dinner parties [v.12].

A PARABLE AT THE PHARISEE'S DINNER [LK.14:15–24]

[15] *A guest at dinner responded, "Happy the one who eats bread in God's kingdom."* [16] *"A man once invited many guests to a great dinner," said Jesus.* [17] *"He sent a servant at the hour of the dinner to tell the guests, 'Come, all is ready.'* [18] *But they begged off. One said, 'I've bought a property I must see. Excuse me.'* [19] *Another said, 'I've bought teams of oxen I must test. Excuse me.'* [20] *Another said, 'I just got married. I can't go.'* [21] *When the servant reported all this, his master was angry. 'Hurry into the streets and alleys of the city. Bring in the poor,*

the disabled, the blind, and the lame.' [22] *After the servant did that, he reported, 'My lord, there's still room.'* [23] *The master said, 'Scour the high roads. Go into the hedges. Tell everyone to come fill my house.* [24] *I say that none of those who were invited first will taste my dinner.'"*

———⁂———

As Luke continues to describe a dinner held at a Pharisee's home on a Sabbath (see 14:1), we hear a guest rhapsodize [v.15] about the heavenly banquet (see Is.55:1; above, 13:29). Luke says Jesus responded to this rather vague expression of hopefulness by describing in some detail how hard God was working to make the heavenly banquet take place.

The parable reported by Luke speaks of one man's great anticipation [vv.16–17] that wasn't shared by any of the people with whom he'd hoped to dine—people whose individual interests had drawn their attention elsewhere [vv.18–20]. It's easy to sympathize with anyone who's said, "Of course I'll be there," and then must say, "Something's come up." But, as Luke depicts him here, Jesus is a teacher who wants to shake up the complacency with which we assign importance to our chosen goals. His parable asks, "What if an invitation or an appeal is desperate and springs from a profound need? What if your God was so eager for your company that he'd risk looking ridiculous as he attempted to get it [v.21]? What if, after God's extraordinary efforts failed to fulfill his hopes for a full kingdom, he kept working until his plan was accomplished? Would you be touched by this God's need, or would you still feel that your concerns were more important than his? If you allowed yourself to be continually distracted by your own interests, would you be surprised if God stopped inviting you to the heavenly banquet?" [vv.22–24].

Chapter 14

FOLLOWING JESUS MEANS ABANDONING ALL ELSE
[LK.14:25–35]

[25] *As Jesus continued toward Jerusalem, great crowds followed. He spoke to them.* [26] *"If anyone comes to me but doesn't hate his father, mother, wife, children, brothers, and sisters—yes, even his own life—he can't be my disciple.* [27] *Whoever doesn't carry his cross and follow along after me can't be my disciple.* [28] *To build a watchtower, don't you first figure how much you need in order to complete it?* [29] *If you lay a foundation but can't finish it, everyone will laugh.* [30] *They'll say, 'This one started to build, but couldn't finish.'* [31] *What king wars with another before figuring if his ten thousand can defeat twenty?* [32] *And, if he figures they can't, he can seek a truce before the twenty thousand arrive.* [33] *So, then, if you don't let go of all you have, you can't be my disciple.* [34] *Look, salt's good. But say it lost its taste. How could it be reseasoned?* [35] *It would be useless as soil or fertilizer. You'd throw it out. You with ears should hear."*

———✵✵✵———

Luke depicts Jesus telling the crowd they must realize that following him—being a disciple—requires more than taking an interest in his words and actions. Luke hasn't presented Jesus as an itinerant expert promoting good behavior and healthy living but as someone who proclaims the need to give up the assumption that we know what's good for us. Luke tells us that, just as Jesus once warned his closest disciples that choosing to repent of selfishness and turning, instead, to God would cost them their deepest prejudices (see 9:23–24), he now explains to a crowd that, to follow his example, they'd have to abandon everything they considered important in life. Indeed, they'd have to give up life itself [vv.25–26]. Letting oneself become free of all self-importance feels like a burden—a cross—says Jesus. But anyone unwilling to experience that burden is also unwilling to following Jesus' example [v.27].

Luke says Jesus used images to stress that, if you're going to make a commitment, you should know what you're getting into. How laughable it is for someone to construct a big basement without knowing if it'll be possible to build anything on top of it [vv.28–30]. What lethal irresponsibility would a ruler be showing to walk into a war—and away from a chance for peace—without knowing the enemy's strength [vv.31–32]. That's how foolish and unthinking are those who assume Jesus doesn't mean what he says when he tells them that following him means walking away from themselves [v.33]. Another image, said Jesus, should make it clear to anyone with ears how sad will be the fate of those who begin discipleship blithely only to abandon it. They'll be as useless as salt that's no longer salty. They'll be nothing but dust [vv.34–35].

FIFTEEN

What Happens to Those Who Get Lost on the Way to God's Kingdom?

HOW DO YOU FEEL WHEN YOU FIND SOMETHING THAT WAS LOST? [LK.15:1–10]

¹ On Jesus' journey to Jerusalem, tariff collectors and sinners came to listen to him. ² Pharisees and scribes complained, "This one welcomes sinners and eats with them." ³ So he told them a parable. ⁴ "Which man among you who owned a hundred sheep, but lost one, wouldn't leave the ninety-nine in the wild to search for the lost one until he found it? ⁵ When he'd found it, he'd happily carry it on his shoulders. ⁶ When he got home, he'd call together his friends and neighbors and say, 'Rejoice with me. I've found my lost sheep.' ⁷ I say that in just that way there'll be more joy in heaven over one repentant sinner than over ninety-nine who are so righteous they need no repentance. ⁸ Which woman among you who had ten silver coins but lost one wouldn't light a lamp and sweep the whole house until she found it? ⁹ When she found it, she'd call together her friends and neighbors to say, 'Rejoice with me. I've found my lost coin.' ¹⁰ I tell you that just so will God's angels rejoice over one sinner who repents."

⚮

Luke tells us that the continued attraction of sinners to Jesus' teaching about repentance prompted the Law's defenders (Pharisees) and scholars (scribes) to make the same complaints Jesus heard at the beginning of his mission (see 5:30). If we picture these particular Pharisees and scribes among those who heard Jesus' warnings about abandoning discipleship (see just above), we can imagine them as doubly indignant: "How can you, who expect your disciples to follow you closely, associate with those who won't even follow the Law!" [vv.1–2].

We hear Jesus trying to enlighten them with his favorite teaching tool [v.3]: parables that invite listeners to reimagine situations they think they already understand. The two parables here [vv.4–10] ask, "Do you always cut your losses? If not, if there are situations in which you go to great trouble to recover something of yours that's gone missing, isn't it possible that God—the God who has promised to care for you (see, e.g., Ex.6:7ff.)—also goes to great trouble to bring you back to him when you've turned away? If joy and relief naturally overwhelm you when you've found something you treasure, and if you instinctively share your pleasure with those around you, isn't it possible that God, like you, can't contain his delight when he's able to regain your attention?" Compare that delight, says Jesus, with the fun of being surrounded by those whose main concern is to make no mistakes [vv.7, 10].

A PARABLE ABOUT THE RELIEF THAT REPENTANCE BRINGS
[LK.15:11–32]

[11] *Jesus told another parable. "A man had two sons.* [12] *The younger said, 'Father, grant me my share of the estate now.' He granted it.* [13] *The young son packed up, traveled far, and wasted his money in dissipation.* [14] *When he'd spent it all, a famine struck that distant place. He was in great need.* [15] *He met a citizen there who sent him to tend pigs.* [16] *He wished he could grub with the pigs. (He wasn't provided with food.)* [17] *It struck him, 'My father's hired hands can leave leftovers, but I'm starving.* [18] *I'll go to my father. I'll say, "I've sinned against heaven and before you.* [19] *I'm not worthy to be called your son. Use me as a hired hand."'*

[20] *So, he went back to the father. The father saw him far away and was overcome by pity. He ran to him, flung his arms around him, and kissed him.* [21] *'Father,' he said, 'I've sinned against heaven and you. I'm not fit to be called—* [22] *But the father told the servants, 'Hurry, get him a fine robe, his ring, and sandals!* [23] *Bring in the fatted calf and slaughter it. We'll feast and be happy.* [24] *This son of mine was dead. He's alive! He was lost. He's found!' They feasted.* [25] *The older son was returning from the fields and heard sounds of music and dancing.* [26] *He asked one of the servants about it.* [27] *'Your brother's back,' he said. 'Your father slaughtered the fatted calf because he's safe.'* [28] *He was angry and wouldn't go into the house. The father came out to coax him in.* [29] *He told his father, 'For years I served and obeyed you, but not even a goat did you kill for me to feast on with friends.* [30] *That one, who wasted the estate on whores, comes back and you give him a feast.'* [31] *'My child,' he said, 'you're always with me. All I have is yours.* [32] *But now we're happy and rejoice. Your brother was dead. He's alive! He was lost, now he's found!'"*

———✏✏✏———

Luke continues to narrate Jesus' response to some Pharisees and scribes who criticized his associating with sinners (see 15:2). Here, he gives us the third parable Jesus told them about the pleasures of finding what was lost. In this parable, both sons are depicted as unaware of their father's love for them. We see that the younger one, despite having been treated with extraordinary generosity by his father [v.12], thought that, because he has fallen into great need, he has to make an attractive offer to get further help [vv.18–19]—an offer he doesn't realize is unnecessary even after he experiences an emotional welcome [vv.20–21]. We see that the elder son, though he has spent more time than his brother with the father and saw how generously his father had originally responded to the younger brother's request for a share of the estate, didn't realize the father considered everything he owned as also belonging to his children [v.31]. Both brothers are depicted thinking they know what they want—food, say [v.17], or a feast with friends [v.29]. However, neither of them seems to know how to get what they want. The father, on the other hand, knows that what he wants is to share his life with his sons [vv.31–32]. And he knows that, to make that possible, he'll always be ready to take them into his presence [v.24]. He'll even chase after them when they are distant [vv.20b, 28b].

SIXTEEN

Do You Know What You Want?

WHERE'S YOUR HEART? [LK.16:1–18]

¹ After telling parables [about forgiveness] to the complaining authorities [see 15:3–32], Jesus told one to his disciples: "A rich man's steward was accused of mismanagement. ² The man said, 'O, I've heard such things about you! You're no longer my steward. Give an account.' ³ The steward worried, 'What else can I do? I can't dig. I'm ashamed to beg. ⁴ I know. I'll find a way to be welcomed in others' houses.' ⁵ He contacted his master's debtors. He asked one, 'How much do you owe?' ⁶ 'A hundred vats of oil,' he said. The steward insisted, 'Write a receipt for fifty.' ⁷ 'What do you owe?' he asked another. 'A hundred bushels of wheat.' 'Put down eighty.' ⁸ The master praised the wily steward for being smart. Indeed, the children of the world are smarter than children of light. ⁹ Learn the ways of the market. When it fails, find welcome in the eternal stalls: ¹⁰ if you're reliable in small things, you'll be reliable in large; if you're false in small things, you'll be false in large; ¹¹ if you can't be trusted with this world's goods, who will give you true wealth; ¹² if you can't be trusted to handle mere commodities, why should you get what's truly yours? ¹³ A servant can't serve two masters. Neither can you serve God and mammon." ¹⁴ The Pharisees who were obsessed with money overheard this and laughed at him. ¹⁵ He said, "You put on a good face, but God sees your hearts and abhors your masks. ¹⁶ Up to John, you heard the Law and the prophets. Now you hear me proclaiming the kingdom of God and pushing everyone to enter it. ¹⁷ But the earth and sky will collapse before one letter stroke of the Law will fade. [18] [For example:] Divorcing to remarry is adultery—as is marrying a divorced person."

—⟶∿∿∿⟵—

Luke says Jesus told the disciples a story about plain dealing. A householder discovered that his steward was mishandling his estate [vv.1–2]. Fearing poverty and heavy labor [v.3], the steward approaches other (possible) employers with the attractive offer of lowering his commission on the sales he'd made on behalf of his old master [vv.4–7]. In effect, he's saying to his customers, "I made a mistake in charging you so much!" The master admired this conversion to honest tactics. Luke says Jesus contrasted such diligence in worldly business to the apathy of God's children for his work [v.8].

We then hear Jesus tell the disciples that, if they hoped to be welcomed in the tents on the eternal fairgrounds, they should first learn to be honest in the marketplace [v.9]. This is advice simple enough for children: if you think it's okay to steal pennies now, you'll wind up in jail later [v.10]. Luke says some Pharisees laughed [v.14] at Jesus' teaching that those who did business without concern for the needs of others [vv.11a, 12a] shouldn't expect God to care for their needs [vv.11b, 12b]. One can't serve oneself (mammon) and God at the same time [v.13]. This teaching isn't new, says Jesus: the scriptures—the Law and prophets—tell us God sees us turn our hearts away from him, and that he wants to turn them back to him. This message about God's concern for us won't change, he says [vv.15–17]. As an obvious example of the timelessness of the Law, Jesus explains that it will always be selfish to put your own needs ahead of the needs of a married partner [v.18].

A PARABLE ABOUT DECIDING WHAT YOU WANT
[LK.16:19–31]

[19] Jesus was still speaking to Pharisees and others [see 15:2]: "There was a rich man who could afford linen and richly dyed cloaks, and could feast every day. [20] A poor man, named Lazarus, languished at his gate. He was covered in sores.

²¹ He'd have taken table scraps, but only dogs approached him, licking his wounds. ²² The poor man died and angels took him to the bosom of Abraham. The rich man died and was buried. ²³ From the horror of Hades the rich man saw Abraham far off, and Lazarus with him. ²⁴ 'Pity me, Father Abraham,' he cried. 'Send Lazarus with a finger dipped in water to cool my tongue. I'm in terrible distress in these flames.' ²⁵ 'My child,' said Abraham, 'you had good things in life, Lazarus had bad. He finds comfort now. You find distress. ²⁶ And there's an abyss between us that keeps us from going back and forth.' ²⁷ 'I beg you,' said the rich man, 'send someone to my father's house. ²⁸ I have five brothers who need to be warned away from this terrible place.' ²⁹ 'They have Moses and the prophets,' said Abraham. 'They should listen to them.' ³⁰ 'No, no,' he said. 'If someone goes to them from the dead, they'll repent.' ³¹ 'If they won't listen to Moses and the prophets,' he said, 'they won't be moved by someone who rises from the dead.'"

———◦○◦———

The parable insists that no miracle will force open someone's heart—not even the resurrection [v.31]. Opening up our hearts and giving attention to something that doesn't already preoccupy us is a choice we must make deliberately, not magically. In Luke's narration of this story, Jesus depicts the ease with which one can avoid this deliberate choice.

A rich man is described attending to the details of his clothing and food [v.19] but ignoring the world at his door [vv.20–21]. Lazarus, who did without the goods of this world, found an eternal good. The rich man found that worldly goods perish, leaving nothing [v.22]. The parable depicts the rich man experiencing this "nothing" as a burning desire to have a tiny taste of water—to resurrect one small pleasure from the life he knew [vv.23–24]. He's reminded, first, that while Lazarus had to seek comfort elsewhere, and found it, he sought his comfort in a passing world, and had it; second, there's a profound difference—an abyss—between the two searches [vv.25–26]. He's also reminded that, if he and his brothers know the scriptures (see Dt.30:11–18), they know how important it is to choose between life and death [vv.27–29]. When he says his brothers need another revelation, he's asked the obvious question: if they've chosen not to learn from the word of God when it comes from Moses and the prophets, why suppose they would listen to God's word when it comes from a vision [vv.30–31]?

SEVENTEEN

Still on the Way to Jerusalem; Still Teaching about Repentance

THE DISCIPLES CONTINUE LEARNING ABOUT REPENTANCE AND FORGIVENESS [LK.17:1–10]

[1] Jesus told his disciples, "People will sin, but woe to the one who misleads them. [2] Better to be cast in the sea with a millstone around your neck than to mislead the least of these. [3] Take care to correct your brother if he sins, and to forgive him if he repents. [4] If seven times a day he does wrong to you, and seven times returns to say, 'I'm repentant,' you must forgive him." [5] The apostles said to the Lord, "Give us more faith." [6] The Lord said, "If you had faith the size of a mustard grain you could say to a sycamore tree, 'Be uprooted and planted in the sea,' and it would obey you. [7] Who tells a servant who returns from plowing or herding, 'Come, recline at table'? [8] He's told, 'Prepare and serve my meal. You may eat when I've finished.' [9] Is the servant thanked for doing what's commanded? [10] So with you. When you've done what's commanded, say, 'We've brought you no profit. We've done what is ours to do.'"

━━━◦⟡◦━━━

Luke tells us that the stories and teachings he's been narrating were addressed to crowds following Jesus on his journey (see 14:25). Here, then, we can imagine Jesus still on the road as he speaks once more about sin and repentance. First, says Luke, he warned his disciples that sinning, like any bad habit, seems unavoidable. But one should prefer drowning over tempting even a fool to sin [vv.1–2]. Second, though selfishness—sin—should be reproved in a fellow believer, repentance must be met by forgiveness [v.3]. Even if you're the victim of selfishness many times a day, you must greet each apology with forgiveness [v.4]. When Luke says the apostles asked for more faith, he may be suggesting they didn't believe they could fulfill the demand for constant forgiving [v.5]. Jesus' response, as Luke reports it, warns that their faith may be even weaker than they think [v.6]. Luke then says Jesus used another image of worldly expectations (compare 16:4–8) to shake up their idea of what God expects of them. In a master-slave relationship, a slave is promised nothing but room and board. In the relationship between God and his children, the children are promised they'll inherit his kingdom. If the apostles assume a slave will do what's expected in return for food and a roof, they should also assume God's children will do what he asks when he commands them to share his desire for repentance, reconciliation, and forgiveness. And when they've acted on God's request that, like him, they should practice graciousness, mercy, and forgiveness, they'll say, "What else would you expect us to do?" [vv.7–10].

HOW GOD'S CARE IS EXPERIENCED BY A LEPER [LK.17:11–19]

[11] Jesus' journey to Jerusalem took him between Galilee and Samaria. [12] Outside one village, there were ten lepers at a distance. [13] They cried, "Jesus, Master, show us compassion." [14] He saw them and said, "Go show yourselves to the priests" [Lv.14:2–9]. As they went, they were made clean. [15] One, seeing he was clean, came back, loudly glorifying God. [16] He was a Samaritan. He fell forward at Jesus' feet and thanked him. [17] Jesus said, "Weren't ten made clean? The other nine, where are they? [18] Why aren't they coming back glorifying God—why only this foreigner? [19] Get up," he said, "and be on your way. Your faith has brought you salvation."

Luke pictures Jesus in a place where he'll meet not only Jews but also Samaritans (a group that believed in the Covenant but not in the need to worship God in Jerusalem) [v.1]. The lepers in this scene had apparently heard of Jesus' reputation for compassion [vv.12–13; see also 7:13; 10:33; 15:20]. As they headed off in response to his command to observe the Law's directions for being declared free of skin infections (see Lv.14:2–9), they discovered they were already freed from their ailment [v.14]—a discovery that caused a man who was a Samaritan to burst into raucous thanksgiving while returning to thank Jesus [vv.15–16]. Luke doesn't describe Jesus as surprised by this noisy display, but as puzzled to see it made by only one of ten [v.17]. If the others were Jewish, why weren't they singing praise to God for fulfilling his promise to care for them [v.18]? The assertion that it was the Samaritan's faith in God's promise that brought him salvation [v.19] suggests that, without such faith, the healing of the others wasn't complete. Though they'd been freed from a skin disease, perhaps they were still enslaved by the cares from which God had been hoping to free them.

JESUS TELLS HIS DISCIPLES HOW TO WATCH FOR THE KINGDOM [LK.17:20–37]

[20] *When some Pharisees asked him when God's kingdom would come, he said, "The kingdom of God won't be seen by watching for signs.* [21] *No one can say, 'Look, it's here!' or 'Look there!' The kingdom of God is in you."* [22] *He told the disciples, "One day, you'll long to see one of the days of the Son of Man, but won't see it.* [23] *They'll say, 'Look there,' or 'Here it is!' Don't rush off looking.* [24] *The day of the Son of Man's coming will be as obvious as lightning across the sky.* [25] *But, first, he must suffer many things and be rejected by this generation.* [26] *As it was in the days of Noah [Gn.6:5ff.], so it will be in the days of the Son of Man.* [27] *They ate, drank, and married the day Noah boarded the ark. The flood killed them.* [28] *So too in Lot's time, they ate, drank, bought, sold, planted, and built.* [29] *And on the day Lot left Sodom, fire and sulfur fell from heaven and killed them.* [30] *The same thing will happen on the day the Son of Man is revealed.* [31] *On*

that day, if you're on the roof, don't run down to collect your things. If you're in the fields, don't run back home. [32] Recall Lot's wife [Gn.19:26]. [33] Those who try to save their lives will lose them. Whoever loses life will keep it. [34] On that night, I tell you, of two in the same bed, one will be taken, the other left. [35] If two are milling grain together, one will be taken, the other left." [[36] Commentators say a line about two people in a field was added later.] [37] But the disciples still asked, "Where?" He said, "Where there's carrion there will be eagles."

—————

Some Pharisees may have heard of the leper's cure (see above, vv.12–19) and wanted to know when God's kingdom would conquer all hurt. Luke says Jesus reminded them that God's kingdom isn't like worldly, visible kingdoms. God wants to rule our hearts [vv.20–21].

Jesus then tells his disciples that, once he's gone, they'll be impatient to see the kingdom [v.22], but that they needn't worry about missing it. It will be obvious when he, the Son of Man, reappears to bring the kingdom to fulfillment [vv.23–24]. Before they can accept God's kingdom, however, they must learn to let go of this worldly realm. Jesus reminds them (see 9:22, 44) he must let himself be stripped of life [v.25], and he cites scripture stories to stress that God continues his work of creation even though many human creatures fixate on the cares of daily life [vv.26–29, 32]. If the disciples want to accept the invitation to enter the kingdom [v.30], they should be ready to leave everything behind without a last look [vv.31–32]; to accept God's life of bliss, one must grow out of this life [v.33]. However, says Jesus, some will cling to the stuff of this life rather than let God take them to himself [vv.34–35].

Despite Jesus' command not to fret about the time or place of the kingdom's arrival, the disciples ask for details about where they might look for signs that God's plan is being fulfilled [v.37a]. Jesus reminds them that, when they catch sight of circling birds of prey, they immediately know there's a carcass out there somewhere. He's telling them, in effect, "When you see the kingdom, you'll recognize it immediately" [v.37b].

EIGHTEEN

How Do You Pray, and What Do You Pray For?

TWO PARABLES ABOUT PRAYING [LK.18:1–14]

¹ Next, Jesus told the disciples a parable about praying constantly but not anxiously. ² "There was once a judge who had no fear of God or anyone else. ³ A widow kept demanding, 'Give me justice against my opponent.' ⁴ After first ignoring her, he thought, 'I don't fear God or anyone else, ⁵ but this widow is trouble. I'll give her justice before she socks me in the eye.'" ⁶ The Lord said, "Listen to the words of the judge who doesn't care what's right. ⁷ Won't God, who does want what's right, sympathize with the cries of his chosen ones? ⁸ I say he'll do what's right quickly. But when the Son of Man comes, will he find anyone believing this?" ⁹ To those who thought they were in the right and everyone else was wrong, he said this. ¹⁰ "Two men went up to the temple to pray: a Pharisee and a collector of Roman taxes. ¹¹ The Pharisee stepped forward and prayed to himself: 'Lord, I give thanks I'm not like others, thieves, liars, adulterers, or like this tariff collector. ¹² I fast twice a week, and I give to the temple 10 percent of all I earn.' ¹³ The tariff collector stood back, didn't look up to heaven, but beat his chest and said, 'God, have mercy on me. I'm a sinner.' ¹⁴ I say he seemed right to God as he walked home, not the other. Those who exalt themselves will be humbled. Those who humble themselves will be exalted."

—⟶∞⟵—

The opposite of worrying about your life (see 17:33a) is to let God take care of it [v.1]. Luke says Jesus used a parable to provoke his disciples to ask themselves if they ever approached God with the same tenacity with which we appeal to someone for something that only they can give us—say, a legal settlement from the district judge. When the disciples need something only God can give, do their hearts ever fail them when they ask for what he's promised [vv.3–7]? Do they imagine that people will ever trust the Father [v.8]?

Luke pictures Jesus turning to a group gathered in one of the towns he's visiting on his way up to Jerusalem (see 17:11). We hear Jesus use another parable to stress that praying is appealing to God for help, not congratulating oneself for needing no help [v.9]. The difference between the characters in the story is obvious: one dedicates himself to defending the Law; the other takes a generous cut from the fees he collects for the occupying Romans [v.10]. The Pharisee can cite his practice of fasting and tithing as proof of his dedication to the Law [vv.11–12]. The man aware of his selfishness has nothing to offer God but his need for forgiveness [v.13]. One way to respond to God's offer of reconciliation, forgiveness, and love is to ignore it—to focus instead on how good one is and to notice how one's good deeds seem to make God's gift of mercy seem unnecessary. Another response is to notice God's offer and grab it out of desperate need: "Help!" According to Luke, Jesus thought only the second was the right way to pray [v.14].

DO PEOPLE KNOW WHAT THEY WANT? [LK.18:15–30]

¹⁵ *When the disciples saw people seeking Jesus' touch for their babies, they objected.* ¹⁶ *"Let the children come," he called out. "Don't stop them. The kingdom is for them.* ¹⁷ *O yes, indeed, I say whoever doesn't greet God's kingdom like a child won't enter it."* ¹⁸ *An official asked, "Good teacher, what must I do to inherit eternal life?"* ¹⁹ *"Why do you call me good?" he asked. "No one's good. Only God is good.* ²⁰ *You know the commandments: 'Do not commit*

adultery; do not kill; do not steal; do not give false witness; honor your father and mother' [Ex.20:12–16]." ²¹ He said, "I've been observing these from my youth." ²² Jesus said, "There's one thing missing. Sell all you have; give the money to the poor; and have your treasure in heaven. Then come follow me." ²³ He was deeply saddened to hear this. He was very rich. ²⁴ Seeing his sadness, Jesus said, "How hard it is for the rich to enter God's kingdom. ²⁵ A camel can go through a needle's eye more easily than a rich person can enter the kingdom of God." ²⁶ His listeners asked, "Who then can be saved?" ²⁷ He said, "What's impossible for human beings is possible for God." ²⁸ Peter said, "Don't forget, we gave up our possessions to follow you." ²⁹ "O yes," said Jesus, "I say anyone who's left home, spouse, siblings, parents, or children for the kingdom of God ³⁰ will receive all that back now, and in the age to come receive eternal life."

Luke says Jesus commented on the disciples' annoyance at baby blessings [v.15] by pointing out that one can enter the kingdom only the way little ones clamor for care [vv.16–17]. The official depicted by Luke seems to think he must prove he's good enough to inherit the kingdom. His use of "good" in addressing Jesus prompts the remark that good is seen only in God, not oneself [vv.18–19]. When we hear that the man has always followed the Covenant's commands to respect others' needs before his own [vv.20–21], we hear Jesus invite him to abandon all concern for himself and leave care in God's hands—an invitation the man doesn't feel free to accept [vv.22–23].

Luke tells us Jesus described the pointlessness of seeking both a worldly kingdom and God's kingdom by painting a ludicrous image [vv.24–25]. Luke then reports a question from the audience that suggests they didn't get Jesus' point, but saw only that he'd described something impossible [v.26]. Yes, says Jesus, it's impossible for anyone to live both in this world and with God—unless helped by God to do so [v.27]. Peter's question suggests he's not sure he *is* getting God's help as he follows Jesus—but that he is sure of his own sacrifices. Jesus' answer notes that the disciples have already found rich new relationships in this world (with fellow disciples) and that they were expecting eternal life [vv.28–30] — weren't they?

HOW DOES ONE RECEIVE GOD'S LIFE? [LK.18:31–43]

³¹ Jesus took the twelve aside and told them, "We're going up to Jerusalem where all that the prophets wrote about the Son of Man will be fulfilled. ³² He'll be handed to the Gentiles to be mocked, reviled, and spat upon. ³³ They'll scourge him and then kill him. And after three days, he'll rise again." ³⁴ They didn't understand. They found his words unclear. They couldn't take it in. ³⁵ As he approached Jericho, a blind man was sitting by the roadside begging. ³⁶ When he heard the passing crowd, he asked what was happening. ³⁷ They told him that Jesus of Nazareth was going by. ³⁸ He cried out, "Jesus, son of David, have mercy on me!" ³⁹ Those in the lead told him to be quiet. But he cried louder, "Jesus, son of David, have mercy on me!" ⁴⁰ Jesus stopped and asked him to come over. Then he asked, ⁴¹ "What do you want me to do?" "Lord," he said, "let me see." ⁴² Jesus said, "Then see once more. Your faith has saved you." ⁴³ At that moment, he saw again. Then he followed Jesus glorifying God. The whole crowd praised God.

In Luke's Gospel, Jesus' references to himself as "the Son of Man" have emphasized that he's a human being doing a particular work—that is, he's a man proclaiming the Good News that God's kingdom gives life. Here, Jesus reminds his disciples that the prophets had written about the violence that would greet anyone who taught that God wants to give us his own life [vv.31–33a]. Nevertheless, says Jesus, this Good News about the gift of life will be proved true by his rising from death [v.33b]. Luke reports that the disciples couldn't quite follow this [v.34].

Luke then describes a blind beggar who seems more aware than the disciples of how God gives life. We hear that Jesus is less than twenty miles east of Jerusalem, heading into Jericho, when a beggar's cries for help clearly imply his belief that Jesus' power to heal makes him the true heir of the powerful King David [vv.35–38].

Luke says those leading the way (perhaps some of Jesus' disciples) couldn't silence the man's insistent hollering [v.39], which led Jesus to inquire about the fuss [v.40]. The simplicity with which Luke narrates the ensuing encounter and its results [vv.41–43] contrasts with the prior hubbub. It's as if to say that getting from one place to another in this life, while also taking care of noisy interruptions, can be confusing and time consuming; but going from hurt to wholeness requires only belief in God's care. Luke says Jesus told the blind man that belief had saved him [v.42b]—that is, freed him not only from physical blindness but also from the anxiety of trying, and failing, to answer all of life's needs for himself. The man agreed, says Luke, and glorified God—an example followed by the crowd [v.43b].

NINETEEN

Why Is Jesus Going to Jerusalem?

¹ Jesus was passing by Jericho on his way to Jerusalem. ² In Jericho, one of the principal tariff collectors was Zacchaeus, a wealthy man. ³ He wanted to get a look at Jesus but, being short, he couldn't see over the crowd. ⁴ He ran ahead and climbed a sycamore to see him passing. ⁵ When Jesus got there and looked up, he said, "Zacchaeus, hurry down. Today I must stay in your house." ⁶ Zacchaeus rushed down and welcomed him to his home with great joy. ⁷ When people saw this they muttered, "He's staying with a sinner." ⁸ Zacchaeus stood to speak to the Lord: "Look, I give half my earnings to the poor, Lord. And if I've demanded too much from someone, I pay it back fourfold." ⁹ Jesus said, "Today, salvation has come to this house. For this too is a child of Abraham. ¹⁰ And the Son of Man has come to seek and save the lost."

⸺◦◦◦⸺

It seems Jesus wasn't going to stop in Jericho [v.1] but decided to do so when he met a man who didn't mind appearing foolish as he energetically sought to see him [vv.2–4]. Luke doesn't say why Jesus invited himself to Zacchaeus' house [v.5], but at this point in the Gospel it's clear that all Jesus' words and actions have one purpose: to preach repentance, reconciliation, forgiveness, and salvation to those who are willing to hear it. Luke suggests that Zacchaeus was delighted at the prospect of savoring Jesus' words during his visit [v.6; see 10:42].

According to Luke, Jesus' desire to spend time with Zacchaeus caused the same disapproval that was aroused by the dinner with Levi (see 5:30). Tariff collectors, who lived off a percentage of the various fees they collected for the Romans, were presumed to be dishonest, and therefore sinful [v.7]. Luke says Zacchaeus described how he tried to do his work honestly, even generously [v.8]. Jesus says that what is happening when Zacchaeus struggles to hear God's word—and to live by it—is simply this: God is working in him to fulfill the promise of salvation (see Gn.12:2–3; 15:1) that he made to Abraham and his children [v.9]. Then we hear Jesus say something similar to what he said at Levi's house (see 5:32): he wants to help people like Zacchaeus keep rediscovering God's promise of salvation [v.10]. This implies that one must desire, as Zacchaeus did, to rediscover it—even if this means looking a bit foolish to others.

WE ARE INVITED TO SHARE GOD'S POWER [LK.19:11–28]

[11] *Because Jesus' listeners thought his approach to Jerusalem meant the kingdom of God was going to appear there immediately, he told a parable.* [12] *"A nobleman went to a distant land to be invested as a vassal king and, after his investiture, to return.* [13] *He summoned ten of his servants and gave them ten gold pieces and told them, 'Conduct business until I come back.'* [14] *While he was gone, some of his fellow citizens who despised him sent a delegation with the complaint: 'We don't want this one to rule over us.'* [15] *Now, when he returned after his investiture, he called for the servants who'd been given money to find out how they'd conducted business.* [16] *The first one reported, 'My lord, I earned ten gold pieces with the one.'* [17] *'Good!' he said. 'You've been reliable with a small thing, take charge of ten towns.'* [18] *A second said, 'With your gold piece, my lord, I earned five.'* [19] *He said to him, 'Take charge of five towns.'* [20] *Another said, 'My lord, here is your gold piece. I kept it wrapped in this cloth.* [21] *Your demands frightened me. I knew you made profits without investing and reaped*

*without sowing.' *²² *'You ornery slave! Your own mouth convicts you: you knew I was demanding. *²³ *Why didn't you put the money in a bank to earn interest until my return? *²⁴ *Take his coin,' he told the attendants. 'Give it to the one with ten.' *²⁵ *'But he already has ten,' they said. *²⁶ *'I say those who have will get more, and the one with nothing will lose even that. *²⁷ *As for my foes who didn't want me as their king, bring them here and execute them.'"* ²⁸ *After Jesus finished speaking, he continued on the way to Jerusalem.*

—◦◦◦—

Although Luke introduces this parable as a response to rumors about the kingdom's imminent arrival [v.11], the parable tells how the kingdom will function, not when it will be fully functional. It's clear from the opening of the story that the nobleman (chosen by some distant, central authority to act as the local king) wants to share his power [vv.12–13]. The rest of the story describes how some accepted a share in his power and some rejected it. Those who accepted the invitation to act like their lord were invited to accept even more of his work and authority [vv.15–19]. One fellow who didn't want to join his lord in his work was relieved of what he'd found burdensome [vv.20–24a]. Luke then describes the king spelling out the obvious to those who objected to giving more to someone with much: whoever showed deep interest in sharing this man's way of working would be given a greater share of his work, and those who were uninterested would be left to their indifference [vv.24b–26]. The story's subplot also concludes neatly: those who wanted to keep this man from returning to their small kingdom [v.14] were themselves cut off from it—completely [v.27]. Luke says Jesus then moved on without any comment [v.28], allowing us to wonder if this story helped the disciples to realize that "sharing God's power" meant sharing the power to bring healing and peace to those who seek it (see 10:5–6).

ARRIVING AT JERUSALEM [LK.19:29–40]

29 Just past Bethphage and Bethany, he stopped on Mt. Olives to send off two disciples. 30 "As you enter that village, you'll find an unbroken colt tied up. Untie it and bring it. 31 If anyone asks why, say, 'The Lord needs it.'" 32 They found things as he described them. 33 As they were untying the colt, its owners asked, "Why are you untying that colt?" 34 They said, "The Lord needs it." 35 They brought it to Jesus, threw their cloaks on it, and helped him up. 36 Others spread their cloaks on the road as he went along. 37 As they began to descend Mt. Olives [toward Jerusalem], the disciples praised God loudly for the miracles they'd seen. 38 They said, "Blessed is the king who comes in the name of the Lord [Ps.118:26]. In heaven, peace; glory in highest heaven." 39 Some Pharisees in the crowd said, "Teacher, silence your disciples!" 40 He said, "If they keep silent, the stones will cry out."

————— ⌇⌇⌇ —————

In this description of Jesus' approach to Jerusalem, Luke says nothing about the people in the city itself. He presents Jesus speaking and acting for the benefit of those who've been traveling with him. (In addition to disciples, perhaps the crowd included pilgrims going to the not-yet-mentioned Passover feast—see below, 22:1.) His fellow travelers hear him send two disciples to collect a specific animal for the simple reason that he needs it [vv.29–31]. Luke's depiction of the disciples carrying out Jesus' directions precisely and without question or comment—even repeating his exact words [vv.32–34]—suggests that the disciples had an inkling that this was the special moment toward which Jesus has been heading (see 9:31, 51; 18:31). Indeed, they attest to the importance of this arrival in Jerusalem by adorning Jesus' mount [v.35], decking his path with their clothes [v.36], giving thanks for the works he's performed [v.37], and proclaiming their belief that his work is the work of God [v.38]. Luke depicts Jesus treating these expressions of joy and gratitude for God's blessings as natural—even necessary. He reports that Jesus told some Pharisees that even senseless rocks have enough sense to rejoice when God is at work [vv.39–40].

GRIEF, DISMAY, AND DANGER [LK.19:41–48]

⁴¹ As Jesus neared the city, he looked at it and wept. ⁴² He said, "If only you knew what would bring you peace today. But you're blinded. ⁴³ A day will come when your enemies will build an encampment around you, surround you, and suffocate you. ⁴⁴ They'll bring you to the ground, Jerusalem, and your children within you. No stone will stand on another, because you didn't recognize the moment of your visitation." ⁴⁵ When Jesus went into the Temple, he started to throw out the merchants there. ⁴⁶ He said, "It's written: 'My house is a house of prayer [Is.56:7], but you make it a bandits' lair [Jer.7:11].'" ⁴⁷ He taught in the Temple every day. But the chief priests, scribes, and the leaders of the people were looking for a way to do away with him. ⁴⁸ However, they found no way to do that while everyone hung on his words.

———◈◈◈———

Luke says a scene of great celebration (see, just above, Jesus' joyful reception into Jerusalem) was followed by a moment of great sorrow—sorrow prompted in Jesus by the thought of all those who refused to share in the rejoicing. He says Jesus expressed this sorrow by imagining the needless collapse of Jerusalem: if only the city and the people in it would recognize the need for God's gift of peace and its presence with them right now [vv.41–42]; how sad it will be if they refuse that peace even when it is present in their midst—that is, in the person of Jesus—and how disastrous will be the result of trying to find peace on their own [vv.43–44]. Luke then gives an example of their blindness to what's important in their lives when he tells us Jesus had to remind them of what they should have learned already from scripture—namely, that the Temple wasn't a place for them to take care of business, but where they were to offer prayers of thanksgiving to God for taking care of them [vv.45–46].

Once Jesus arrived in Jerusalem, Luke tells us, he did what he had always done—he taught. But we hear, once again (see 11:53–54), that some were so offended by his teaching that their only reaction was to think of ways to get rid of him [v.47]. Luke concludes this section with a paradoxical note: the same teaching that filled some officials with fury filled other people with fascination [v.48].

TWENTY

Arguments in the Temple about God's Power to Save

CAN YOU BE SAVED IF YOU THINK YOU'RE ALREADY RIGHTEOUS? [LK.20:1–8]

¹ As Jesus taught people in the Temple later that week, chief priests, scribes and elders came up to him. ² They said, "Tell us what authority you have for doing these things. Who gave you such authority?" ³ "I'll ask you a question," he said. "Answer this. ⁴ Was John's baptism heavenly or human?" ⁵ They thought, "If we say 'heavenly,' he'll ask, 'Why didn't you believe him?' ⁶ If we say, 'human,' the people will stone us since they think he was a prophet." ⁷ So, they said they didn't know its source. ⁸ "Then I won't tell you by whose authority I do these things," said Jesus.

Though Luke doesn't tell us what Jesus was teaching in the Temple [v.1], we assume it was the same message he'd been proclaiming all along: "Repent, be reconciled with God, and be welcomed into his kingdom." The question about authority that Luke says Jesus was asked by Temple officials (priests), scholars of the Law (scribes), and some leaders of the Jerusalem community (elders) indicates either they hadn't heard or hadn't believed anything about Jesus'

121

powerful words and works—beginning with his presentation of himself for baptism (see 3:21–22). From the start of this Gospel, Luke has told us that God's power and authority would reside in Jesus (see 1:32–33) and that Jesus did indeed allow himself to be moved and led by God's Spirit (see, e.g., 4:1). He's also told us that some Jewish leaders didn't believe God was at work in their lives (see 7:30) and that Jesus wanted to let his belief stand in stark contrast to such unbelief (see 9:22)—a stance that would lead to his death, but would also reveal that God was at work in him, and in us.

Luke reports that some of Jerusalem's leaders and officials were unable to have a simple conversation with Jesus [vv.3–4] because they couldn't admit they didn't believe in the teaching of John (or of Jesus) about repentance [vv.5–7]. They seem blind to the fact that their cagey dodging around the truth was not the right way to defend or observe the Law—blind to the fact that their self-righteousness and arrogance were attitudes that called for repentance and healing (see 5:31–32). And if they saw no need for repentance, what would Jesus have to say to them [v.8]?

A PARABLE ABOUT IGNORING GOD'S PLAN TO SHARE HIS KINGDOM [LK.20:9–19]

⁹ Jesus told this parable to the people [and to the officials who had questioned his teaching in the Temple]. "A man planted a vineyard, leased it, and took a long journey. ¹⁰ At harvest, he sent a servant to collect his share. But the servant was beaten and sent off. ¹¹ He sent another servant. He too was beaten, abused, and then sent off. ¹² He sent a third who was also tortured and sent away. ¹³ The owner thought, 'What should I do? Maybe they'll respect my beloved son.' ¹⁴ But the tenants said, 'Here's the heir. Let's kill him and take his inheritance.' ¹⁵ So they dragged him out of the vineyard and killed him. What will that owner do? ¹⁶ He'll come and slay those tenants and give others the vineyard." "Oh, no!" said the people listening. ¹⁷ "Yes!" he said. "What does this scripture mean: 'The stone rejected by the builders has become the cornerstone' [Ps.118:22]? ¹⁸ Those who fall against that stone will break apart. Those on whom it falls will be crushed." [19] The scribes and chief priests wanted to lay hold of him right then because they saw the parable was meant for them. But they feared the people.

—————◦/◦/◦/————

After showing us how some Jerusalem officials and leaders resisted a discussion about repentance (see just above), Luke now shows Jesus describing the effects of such resistance by telling a story about arrogance [vv.9–16a]. All Jesus' parables nudge listeners to consider something that seems obvious to them (for instance, that diseased fruit indicates a problem with a tree) but also to ask themselves whether it reveals a truth they're ignoring (say, that the yearnings of their hearts are murky). Such a simple act of the imagination can lead to insight: "Oh, I see!" This parable, however, elicits gasps of "Oh, no!" [v.16b]—the natural response toward which the story builds: "The tenants did *what*?" "The owner thought *what*?" "And then the tenants did *that*!" The final "Oh, no!" suggests that the audience couldn't imagine how anyone could behave as foolishly as the tenants described in the parable—surely religious authorities wouldn't behave that way! But Luke says Jesus reminded his listeners the scriptures told them that anyone (even experts) can make such foolish choices [v.17]. The addition of two other images about a cornerstone stresses the deadly results of assuming that one's plans are better than God's plans [v.18].

According to Luke, the authorities were touched by this parable. But it moved them to fury, not reflection. However, they again decided to be secretive (see 20:5–7) and not reveal their feelings or impulses [v.19]. Luke will tell us how their deviousness led to more and more deviousness—starting in the next scene.

DO YOU HAVE TO OPPOSE EARTHLY POWER TO SERVE GOD?
[LK.20:20–26]

[20] The authorities, hoping to put a stop to Jesus, monitored him as he taught in the Temple. They sent informers who, pretending to be pious, tried to make him say something for which he could be handed over to the Roman governor.

²¹ These informers said, "Teacher, we know you speak and teach what's correct. You flatter no one. You teach only the truth—the way of God. ²² Are we permitted, according to the Law, to give tax money to Caesar, or not?" ²³ He saw their trap. ²⁴ "Show me one of the silver coins," he said. "Whose image and saying is here?" "Caesar's," they said. ²⁵ "Then give Caesar's things to Caesar, and the things of God to God." ²⁶ They failed to trap him in front of the people with his own words. His answer surprised them into silence.

This story indicates the determination of certain authorities in Jerusalem to put an end to Jesus and his teaching [v.20]. But it also demonstrates Jesus' intention to keep teaching what he's always taught: we belong to God [v.25]. The pious poseurs sent by the authorities are described as pretending to be obsequious [v.21], then getting to the point of their trap. They seem to hope that the people who'd been hanging on Jesus' words (see 19:48) would now hear him say either that he agreed with the foreign tax (which could cause an uproar of disagreement between those who felt it was prudent to pay fees levied by a conqueror, and those who thought it was wrong) or that he was opposed to it (which could lead the Roman authorities to accuse him of sedition) [v.22]. Luke says Jesus, seeing through this flattery and ruse [v.23], borrowed a common silver coin—a denarius—that was stamped with the emperor's image and an inscription proclaiming his augustness—facts familiar to all in the crowd [v.24]. Jesus then points out two things known to everyone listening [v.25]. First, the coin belonged to Caesar (who could, say, recall, recast, or devalue it). Second, as a scribe once told Jesus when asked (see above, 10:26–27), those who accept scripture's description of the Law and the Covenant know they belong to God with all their heart, being, strength, and mind (see Dt.6:5). Coins have nothing to do with their minds, hearts, or inner being. And if, like Jesus, they're willing to allow themselves to be taken up completely by God, they won't have any trouble parting with loose change.

According to Luke, everyone in the scene seemed to understand and accept these truths—or they simply had no stomach to contradict them. So there wasn't anything left to say [v.26].

WHOSE PLAN WILL GOD FOLLOW IN ORDER TO SAVE US?
[LK.20:27–40]

²⁷ *Sadducees came to question him. (They didn't believe in the resurrection.)* ²⁸ *"Teacher," they said, "Moses wrote, 'If a man's brother dies childless, he's to marry the wife [Dt.25:5]—to raise children for his brother' [Gn.38:8]. ²⁹ Now, the first of seven brothers married a woman, but died childless. ³⁰ Then the second married her. ³¹ Then the third, then each of the others—all seven dying childless. ³² Finally, the woman died. ³³ So, at the 'resurrection,' whose wife will she be?"* ³⁴ *Jesus said, "The children of this age marry. ³⁵ But those found worthy to enter the age of resurrection from the dead don't marry. ³⁶ Because they can no longer die, they're like angels. As children of the resurrection, they are children of God. ³⁷ Even Moses, in the story about the burning bush, spoke of the dead rising. He called the Lord, 'the God of Abraham, the God of Isaac, the God of Jacob' [Ex.3:6]. ³⁸ He's not the God of the dead, but of the living! To him, all are alive."* ³⁹ *Some scribes who heard this answer said, "Nicely put, Teacher."* ⁴⁰ *And they didn't dare ask him any more questions.*

———⟨৩/৩/৩⟩———

Here Luke introduces some Sadducees, members of a group that promoted a strict reading of scripture—in which they found no mention of resurrection [v.27]. Luke's report of their presentation of a theoretical case reads like a challenge, not an invitation to dialogue. True, Luke doesn't say these Sadducees were trying to trap Jesus. But the clinical coolness with which they use the Law of Moses to pile up bodies in their story and then ask Jesus to find a suitable resurrected husband among them suggests they hope their audience will find their clever ridicule of Jesus amusing [vv.28–33]. Jesus' answer implies the question: "Do you imagine things can happen only as you see them happening in this world?" Yes, he tells them, at this moment—or in this age—we see people marrying [v.34], but what if that won't always be so [v.35]?

Luke says Jesus proclaimed his belief that God wouldn't let death—or any other non-angelic limit of this world—be the final disposition of his children's lives [v.36]. We then hear him remind them of what they knew from scripture: Moses didn't call upon a God of the dead [v.37]. If, then, all the children of God are alive in his eyes, where else would they be, after their deaths in this life, but resurrected from that death into the life of God [v.38]?

Luke's narrative lets us imagine that some scribes [v.39] were not trying to silence Jesus (cf. 20:19), then tells us that Jesus was free, for now, to teach in the Temple [v.40].

WHAT DO PEOPLE HOPE THE FULFILLMENT OF GOD'S PLAN WILL LOOK LIKE? [LK.20:41–47]

⁴¹ Jesus asked the people listening to his teaching in the Temple, "How can anyone say, 'The Messiah is the son of David'? ⁴² David himself said in the Book of Psalms, 'The Lord said to my lord, "Sit at my right hand. ⁴³ I'll make your enemies a footstool for you"' [Ps.110:1]. ⁴⁴ If David calls him 'my lord,' how can he be his son?" ⁴⁵ Then, for everyone to hear, he spoke to his disciples. ⁴⁶ "Watch out for scribes who parade around in long robes and love deferential bowing in the marketplace, prime seats in the synagogue, and high places at banquets. ⁴⁷ They gobble up the goods of widows and like to seem lost in prayer. They'll get a harsh judgment."

Earlier in this Gospel, Luke described Jesus telling others not to speak of him as the Messiah, God's Anointed One (see 4:41; 9:21–22). Here, Luke says Jesus corrected anyone who tried to identify the Messiah without understanding what the Messiah's role was [v.41]. David had been chosen and anointed through God's intervention (see 1 Sm.16:12–13), and he built a great kingdom—which was later conquered. But we hear Jesus discourage the hopes of anyone who wanted a powerful king to rise from David's line and be anointed by God to restore Israel to its former glory. Such an expectation, he says, is much too low—as the composer of the Psalms realized. Luke depicts Jesus using the convention that David wrote the Psalms and noting that David imagined God, "the Lord," giving power over all destructive forces to his, David's, *lord*—that is, someone greater than a mere earthly king [vv.42–44]. The lesson is that the children of God should expect more from the Messiah than worldly power.

Next, Luke says Jesus warned his disciples [v.45] against seeking worldly praise. If we picture the approving scribes (see above, v.39) still in the crowd, we have to wonder if they nodded approvingly when they heard these comments about their ambitions. For Luke says Jesus wanted his disciples to beware the desire for celebrity and fame. How seductive are the admiring stares of those who flatter our wisdom and goodness—who always defer to us and give us special attention [v.46]. But watch out, says Jesus. Those who feel important because of their success in appearing righteous will also fool themselves into thinking that religiosity can hide a rapacious heart [v.47a]. If God sees what's in our hearts, what judgment is he likely to make about a heart that gives itself over to a greedy, grasping pursuit of sanctimoniousness [v.47b]?

TWENTY-ONE

Teaching in the Temple about Expecting God's Kingdom

A WIDOW PLACES EVERYTHING IN GOD'S CARE [LK.21:1–4]

¹ Jesus looked up and saw the wealthy putting offerings into the Temple treasury. ² He also saw a poor widow put in two tiny coins. ³ He said, "Truly, I tell you, that poor widow put in more than all the rest. ⁴ They made offerings from spare funds. She, in her neediness, offered all she had."

———⟡———

Luke just described Jesus instructing people in the Temple to have higher hopes than personal power and fame. Here he tells us Jesus encouraged his followers to put their trust in something greater than what can be seen (see also 21:45). They hear him contrasting some rich folks with a poor widow. The rich contribute some of their funds to support the upkeep of the Temple building. But the widow—who apparently has no relatives upon whom she can rely for financial help—gives her few funds as a gift. Her gift gave witness to her trust in something greater than the Temple [vv.1–4]. In other words, by putting her future—her whole self—in God's hands, she "put in more than all the rest" [v.3].

Chapter 21

WHAT WILL HAPPEN WHILE YOU WAIT FOR THE KINGDOM?
[LK.21:5–19]

⁵ When some mentioned the Temple's fine stonework and votive offerings, Jesus said: ⁶ "A day will come when all you see here will be torn down—no stone left on another." ⁷ "Teacher," they said, "When will this be, and what will be the warning signs?" ⁸ "Don't let yourselves be deceived," he said. "Many will come in my name saying, 'Here I am; the time comes near!' Don't chase after them.
⁹ When you hear about wars and revolutions, don't panic. This sort of thing must happen first. But that's not the ending." ¹⁰ Then he told them, "Nation will rise against nation, kingdom against kingdom. ¹¹ Everywhere there will be earthquakes, famines, and plagues, and the sky will fill with dazzling, terrifying signs.
¹² But before these things happen, you will be attacked and harassed. They'll haul you before synagogues and into prisons; they'll drag you before kings and governors—all because of my name. ¹³ This will lead to you giving witness.
¹⁴ Keep your hearts tranquil. You don't have to practice a defense. ¹⁵ I'll give you a voice and wisdom that your adversaries will not be able to resist or contradict.
¹⁶ Yes, even your parents, siblings, relatives, and friends will betray you. Some of you will be executed. ¹⁷ All will hate you because of my name. ¹⁸ But not a hair on your head will be lost. ¹⁹ It's by persisting in life that you have life.

———∞∞———

If the remark Luke reports about the Temple's beauty [v.5] was an attempt to change the subject from trust in God (see just above) to admiration of human handiwork, it failed. For Jesus reminds his listeners they can't trust worldly splendor [v.6]. Luke says this remark prompted the disciples to ask (anxiously?) what the warning signs of the Temple's collapse would be [v.7]. In answer, we hear Jesus first mention some things about which they need not concern themselves: anyone who pretends to speak in his name about the end times [v.8]; how the world's violence will build to a climax [v.9]; and natural disasters and other frightening phenomena [vv.10–11]. Then Jesus tells them what they should attend to. They should be prepared for the fact that, whenever they act in his name, they'll provoke others to demand an explanation [v.12]. When this happens, they should testify that they believe in Jesus' message [v.13], but they need not plan an elaborate defense of his teaching [v.14]. Jesus promises to give them his own wisdom when they share his message [v.15].

True, Jesus' simple message (of repentance and forgiveness) won't lead to the kind of acclaim sought by some people (see 20:46), and even those closest to the disciples may reject the message violently [v.16]. In fact, the disciples are likely to encounter lethal animosity everywhere [v.17]. This threat to their lives should not distress them (see 6:22). Rather, they should remember that it is God who gives life, and they should keep asking for more of that gift [vv.18–19].

PREPARING FOR THE IMMEDIATE FUTURE; PREPARING FOR REDEMPTION [LK.21:20–38]

[20] *When you see Jerusalem surrounded by armies, that's when destruction is near.* [21] *Those in Judea should flee to the mountains; those in the city should leave it; those outside it should not go back.* [22] *These are the days of recompense [see Hos.9:7], when all scripture will be fulfilled.* [23] *How sad it will be for those pregnant and nursing in that day of earth's distress, the day of wrath for this people.* [24] *They'll be slain by the sword and enslaved in foreign lands. Jerusalem will be overrun by pagans until the season of pagan rule is over.* [25] *A time will come when signs will appear in the sun, moon, and stars. People will wonder at the roaring of the sea.* [26] *They'll faint from fear of what's to happen, for they'll think the power of heaven has collapsed.* [27] *Then they'll see the Son of Man on a cloud, coming to them with great glory.* [28] *When this starts to happen, stand up, lift your heads, for your redemption is near."* [29] *Then he told this parable. "Look at the fig tree, or any other tree.* [30] *When its leaves sprout, your eyes tell you summer is near.* [31] *So, when you see these things, know the kingdom of God is near.* [32] *O, yes indeed, I say this generation won't pass away until these things happen.* [33] *This heaven and the earth will pass away, but my words won't pass away.* [34] *Don't let that day find your hearts muddled by pleasure, drink, or daily worries.* [35] *It will spring like a trap, startling all who live on the face of the earth.* [36] *Always watch. Pray to avoid such things; then, stand before the Son of Man."*

³⁷ Each day, Jesus would teach in the Temple, and spend the night on Mt. Olives. ³⁸ In the morning, all the people would rise early to listen to him in the Temple.

———*o/o/o*———

Luke says Jesus depicted the destruction of Jerusalem [v.20] as a consequence of people repeating the mistakes made in the time of Hosea (when the city was treated merely as a place of business, not a place of worship) [v.22]. Who wouldn't flee [v.21] the horror of being a mother caught in a place where war is preferred to divine forgiveness [v.23]? How sad to choose death and devastation [v.24a] rather than God's peace (see 19:42). Pagan self-interest will flourish in a city where people no longer gather to thank God for his graciousness, mercy, and love [v.24b].

We then hear that, when signs of cosmic change appear, every sound and motion may make people so anxious they'll think God has abandoned creation [vv.25–26]. But the final moment will reveal the glory of Jesus—the perfect Son of Man, who puts his trust in God [v.27]. This is a time to yearn for, not to dread (cf. 17:22ff.)—a time when people will no longer resist God's desire for a Covenant with them [v.28]. It will be as easy to recognize this time of our deliverance as it is to notice the arrival of summer [vv.29–30]. What surrounds us now will give way to a new creation [v.31]. Yes, we'll see the things of this world die [v.32], but we should know that Jesus' teaching will not die; it will prove true [v.33]. We should avoid distraction [v.34] lest the triumph of Jesus' truth burst upon us as a shock [v.35]. Ask the Father for help against distraction [v.36; see 11:4]. Despite the unsettling parts of this message, Jesus kept teaching it. And some people who heard it kept listening [vv.37–38].

TWENTY-TWO

Jesus Celebrates Passover with His Disciples; He Is Arrested

TWO DIFFERENT PREPARATIONS FOR THE FEAST [LK.22:1–13]

¹ The Feast of Unleavened Bread, called the Passover, was approaching. ² At that time, the chief priests and scribes, fearing the people, sought to kill Jesus. ³ Satan entered Judas, called Iscariot, one of the twelve. ⁴ Judas spoke to the chief priests and Temple guards about handing Jesus over to them. ⁵ Delighted, they promised to pay him in silver. ⁶ After this pact, he pondered how best to hand him over without a crowd present. ⁷ The day of Unleavened Bread arrived— the day to sacrifice the Passover lamb. ⁸ Jesus told Peter and John, "Make preparations for us to eat the Passover meal." ⁹ "Where shall we prepare it?" they asked. ¹⁰ He said, "When you enter the city, a man with a water jug will meet you. Follow him into the house he enters. ¹¹ Tell the master of the house, 'The Teacher says, "Where's the guest room where my disciples and I may eat the Passover?"' ¹² He'll show you a large, furnished, upstairs room. Prepare it there." ¹³ Off they went and found things just as he said. They prepared the Passover there.

Earlier, Luke said Jesus was intent on going to Jerusalem to give himself completely to the Father (see 9:22, 51)—a purpose the disciples didn't understand (see 9:45). Here he tells us Jesus continued to lay out his plans to his disciples, as the Jerusalem authorities continued to plan for his destruction (see 20:20) — even though it was during the feast of Passover [vv.1–2], a feast that celebrated God's power to save his children from destruction (see Ex.20:2). Jesus had been tempted to seek power for himself (see 4:6) but turned away from it. Luke tells us Judas succumbed to this temptation and worked out a deal with the authorities to satisfy their shared lust for having their own way [vv.3–5] — though all of them feared having their desires discovered [vv.2b, 6].

Luke describes Jesus arranging for this moment with great care: Peter and John were sent off with detailed instructions that led to a specific place in which Jesus wanted to celebrate this feast with his disciples [vv.7–12]. Like the disciples who'd been sent to fetch a colt (see 19:30), Peter and John executed their task without demanding explanations, apparently trusting (for once) that Jesus knew exactly what he was doing. And things did indeed turn out just as he'd explained [v.13].

If this were a play, most of this description could be considered stage directions for getting from one scene to the next. But it's a narrative that tells us how clearly Jesus moved toward his desire while Judas and others worked in the dark to thwart him.

JESUS EXPLAINS HIS DESIRE TO HIS DISCIPLES [LK.22:14–23]

[14] When the hour had come, he reclined at table with the apostles. [15] He said, "How deeply I've wanted to eat this Passover with you before I suffer. [16] I tell you I won't eat it again until its promise is fulfilled in the kingdom of God." [17] He took a cup, gave thanks, and said, "Take this and share it among you. [18] I tell you I won't drink the fruit of the vine again until the kingdom of God comes." [19] Then he took bread, gave thanks, and gave it to them, saying, "This is my body that's given for you. Do this in remembrance of me." [20] In the same way, with the cup after eating, he said, "This cup is the new covenant in my blood poured out for you. [21] But imagine, the hand of the one who will hand me over is with me at table. [22] The Son of Man proceeds as God plans, but woe to the man who betrays

him." *23 They started to argue with one another which of them could do such a thing.*

——————∽◍∽——————

Luke has consistently depicted Jesus' work as teaching. Here, he describes Jesus using the Passover meal to attempt once more to instruct his closest disciples about his intense desire to place himself completely in the Father's hands—even though that will lead to his rejection, suffering, and death [vv.14–15]. This desire, he tells them, will also lead him to the glory of God's kingdom, though it will mean the end of his eating and drinking in this world [vv.16–18]. Luke records no response to what, by now, should be a familiar lesson (see 9:22, 44; 18:31–33).

Neither does Luke record the apostles' response when Jesus asked them to let him be in their presence when they broke bread with one another as he was doing—an act of giving himself to them [v.19]. Nor does Luke report their response when, after the Passover meal—in which they celebrated God's Covenant of care for his children—Jesus asked them to drink a cup that celebrated a new Covenant—the Covenant that the prophet Jeremiah hoped for (Jer.31:31)—in which Jesus leads the way in accepting God's promise of care [v.20].

Though Luke told us earlier that Jesus named twelve of his disciples "apostles"—that is, men "given a commission" (see 6:13)—and that he shared with them his power to heal the bedeviled and the sick (see 9:1), Luke also told us the apostles had doubts about Jesus' teaching (see 17:5–6). Now, when the apostles hear one of them will turn completely away from Jesus' teaching by betraying him [v.21], they want to guess which of them could be so undone by doubts and misgivings [v.23]. They say nothing in response to Jesus' statement that he wants to let God's plan of creation come to perfection, and that he sees the sad paradox of that plan unfolding through wickedness [v.22].

Chapter 22

JESUS TRIES TO EXPLAIN POWER TO HIS DISCIPLES
[LK.22:24–38]

²⁴ Next, at their dinner, the disciples got into an argument about who seemed greatest. ²⁵ He said, "Pagan kings lord it over others; power brokers like to be called 'benefactors.' ²⁶ Not so with you. Let the greatest be like the youngest; let the leader be the servant. ²⁷ Who seems greater, the one at table, or the one serving table? Is it the one dining? But I serve! ²⁸ Now, you're the ones who've stayed with me during my time of testing. ²⁹ I give you a kingship of the sort my Father has given me. ³⁰ Eat, drink at my table in my kingdom; sit on thrones judging Israel's twelve tribes. ³¹ Simon! Watch out, Simon; Satan wants to toss all of you like wheat. ³² I pray you won't lose faith. But, when you do, repent to encourage your brothers. ³³ "Lord," said Peter, "I'm ready to go to prison, to death, for you." ³⁴ "Peter," he said, "I say you'll deny me three times today before the cock crows." ³⁵ Then he said, "When I sent you off without money bag, sack, or sandals, did you need anything?" "No," they said, "nothing." ³⁶ He said, "But now, hold on to your money bag or sack; and if you have no sword, sell your cloak and buy one. ³⁷ I tell you, this scripture must find its full meaning in me: 'He let himself be taken for a sinner' [Is.53:12]. All that concerns me now comes to fulfillment." ³⁸ "Lord," they said, "look: two swords!" "Enough of that," he said.

———— ✧✧✧ ————

Here Luke describes another argument about rank (cf. 9:46) erupting after the dispute about the betrayer (see above, v.23). It's as if they argued, "I couldn't be a betrayer; look at the great work I've done" [v.24]. Luke says Jesus told the apostles only nonbelievers thought that rank demanded deference and that beneficence trickled down from power [v.25]. If he, Jesus, was a servant, so must his disciples be [vv.26–27]. They'd seen that, when others tested his resolve to do God's will, he kept teaching about God's promise of the kingdom. If they followed his example of persistence, they too would inherit the kingdom, ruling and judging along with him over a new Israel made up of those who accepted, as he did, the need to turn to God in all things [vv.28–30].

Luke says Jesus told them repentance would be a constant necessity—especially for Simon and the rest of the apostles—and that its celebration was a powerful witness [vv.31–32]. (Recall what happened after Jesus' baptism—see 3:21–22.) Luke's description of Simon Peter's response reveals how little Peter understood his need to turn to God rather than to depend on himself [vv.33–34].

Then we hear Jesus tell the apostles that, although at first they needed nothing but willingness to proclaim the kingdom (see 9:1–6), if they wish to continue, they should be ready for hardship and danger [vv.35–36]. After a last reminder that his mission is to fulfill God's promise to send someone who understood sin and could free others from it, Jesus says his mission is nearing its completion [v.37]. And they once more misunderstand him [v.38].

JESUS PRAYS AND IS ARRESTED [LK.22:39–53]

[39] *As usual, Jesus left the city for Mt. Olives, followed by his disciples.* [40] *When he arrived, he said, "Pray that you don't give in to temptation."* [41] *He then walked a stone's throw away, knelt, and prayed:* [42] *"Father, if you want, take this cup from me; but let it be your will, not mine."* [[43] *An angel appeared to him from heaven to strengthen him.* [44] *In agony, he prayed more intensely, his sweat dripping like blood on the ground.]* [45] *He got up from prayer, went to the disciples, and found them groggy with grief.* [46] *"Why are you napping?" he asked. "Pray not to give in to temptation."* [47] *As he spoke, a crowd came, lead by Judas, one of the twelve, who went to kiss him.* [48] *And Jesus said, "Judas, you hand over the Son of Man with a kiss?"* [49] *When his followers saw this, they asked, "Lord, shall we strike with the sword?"* [50] *And one of them slashed the high priest's servant, slicing off the right ear.* [51] *"Stop," said Jesus. He touched the man's ear and healed him.* [52] *He then spoke to the chief priests, Temple police, and elders in the crowd: "Did you come with swords and clubs to protect yourselves against a hooligan?* [53] *I was with you every day in the Temple and you didn't lift a finger against me. But this is your moment—the time for darkness to rule."*

———

Luke tells us Jesus and the disciples slept on Mt. Olives (see 21:37). Returning there this night [v.39], Jesus tells his disciples to pray as he taught them (see 11:4); then he does the same [vv.40–41]. He's described as *wanting* the Father to desire what he, Jesus, desires (cf. 4:3–12) but *asking* that it be the other way around [v.42]. The sentences labeled vv.43–44 may not be Luke's composition, but they suit the narrative inasmuch as they depict a messenger from God helping Jesus continue his struggle to accept the Father's plan of creation as it unfolds in what seems like a painful defeat. Luke then describes Jesus finding that his disciples have stopped their struggle with God's will by falling asleep instead of praying for help in their temptations [vv.45–46].

Jesus' words to them about prayer are interrupted by a crowd whose shady business is begun with false affection—a kiss [v.47]—to which Jesus responds with a question that expresses the truth [v.48]. The disciples' impulsive and violent reaction reveals they haven't understood Jesus' instructions (see 22:38). Their bluster is both comical [v.49] and dangerous [v.50]. Luke describes Jesus' impulse in the situation as the same as it's been in other situations: he heals [v.51]. Jesus is also described as confronting the crowd with the truth about their actions: they couldn't act openly against him because they have nothing with which to charge him. Unlike a dangerous criminal, he's done nothing more than teach. But this is the hour—the time before God's plan comes to fulfillment—when dark deeds can seem to triumph [vv.52–53].

DENIAL; CONDEMNATION [LK.22:54–71]

[54] *The crowd seized him and took him to the house of the high priest. Peter followed.* [55] *When some people lit a fire in the courtyard and sat around it, Peter joined them.* [56] *A maid saw him by the fire, stared, and said, "This one was with him."* [57] *He denied it: "Ma'am, I don't know him."* [58] *Later, another saw him and said, "You're with them." "No, I'm not," he said.* [59] *An hour later someone insisted, "He must have been with him—he's Galilean."* [60] *"Sir," said Peter, "I don't know what you're speaking of." Then, the cock crowed.* [61] *The Lord turned*

and looked at Peter, who then remembered the Lord's words, "You will deny me three times today before the cock crows." [62] Peter left and wept bitterly. [63] Those who kept Jesus captive ridiculed and beat him.

[64] They had blindfolded him, and they said, "Prophesy! Who hit you?" [65] And they offered many other insults. [66] At dawn, the elders, chief priests, and scribes brought him before their Sanhedrin. [67] They said, "Tell us if you're the Messiah." He said, "You won't believe if I say so. [68] And if I question you, you won't respond. [69] But now the Son of Man will sit at the right hand of the power of God." [70] "So, you're the son of God?" they asked. He said, "You're saying I am." [71] "We've heard it from his own mouth!" they said. "We need no more testimony."

—◦◦◦—

Luke describes the work of darkness mentioned by Jesus (see above, v.53) being carried out—and Peter following him [v.54] in a manner quite different from the one envisioned when he was first called (see 5:10–11). Next, a seemingly cozy setting turns tense with an implicit accusation [vv.55–56]. We read above that Jesus told his disciples to acknowledge him (see 12:8–10), and that Peter swore to be faithful to him (see 22:33). Here Peter turns down the opportunity to fulfill his promise [v.57]—and also rejects two other chances [vv.58–60]. Luke, who seems to picture Jesus either in the courtyard or passing through it, tells us a look was all Peter needed to recall Jesus' warning [v.61]—a recollection that brought tears of regret and repentance [v.62].

According to Luke, Jesus' captors, while waiting for the workaday business of bringing him to trial, dithered away the night with cruelty [vv.63–65]. And when the time for official business arrived [v.66], the complete assembly of all officials, the Sanhedrin, adopted a businesslike pose—a pretension Jesus challenges [vv.67–68]. Then, though Jesus tells his accusers they're incapable of discussing the role of God's Anointed One—the Messiah—he also says they will indeed see him, the Son of Man who fully accepts God's plan for humanity, sharing God's power [v.69]. Jesus then points out the irony of the authorities' question: "Yes, you've hit on the exact truth" [v.70]. But they rejected the possibility of that truth [v.71].

TWENTY-THREE
Arranging and Achieving a Death

SOME ADMINISTRATIVE FUN [LK.23:1–12]

¹ Those who had assembled [see 22:66] got up and brought Jesus to Pilate.
² They brought this accusation: "We found this one misleading our people—speaking against the tax to Caesar, and calling himself 'Messiah,' a king!"
³ Pilate asked, "Are you the king of the Jews?" "You're saying this," he said. ⁴ "I find no guilt in this man," said Pilate to the chief priests and the gathered crowd.
⁵ They insisted, "From Galilee to here in Judea, his teaching is inciting the people." ⁶ Pilate asked if the man was a Galilean. ⁷ Hearing he was in Herod's jurisdiction, he sent him to Herod, who was in Jerusalem. ⁸ Herod, who'd wanted to meet Jesus, was delighted to meet him—hoping to see a miracle. ⁹ He asked many questions, but got no answer from Jesus. ¹⁰ All the while, the chief priests and scribes stood there making angry accusations. ¹¹ Herod and his officers, with insults and ridicule, threw a splendid cloak on him and sent him back to Pilate.
¹² Herod and Pilate became friends that day, though they had been adversaries.

—————

Although the Jewish officials who'd arrested Jesus are described as intent on presenting their case [v.1] and willing to fake evidence [v.2], Pilate seems interested only in the charge of claiming kingship [v.3a]. But when Jesus shows no sign of seeking power [v.3b], Pilate

141

tells the authorities—and the crowd that had gathered to watch—
there was no case [v.4]. Luke says Pilate dealt with further fulmina-
tions by delegating the matter to a local ruler, whose family had
kept its rights to govern by pledging allegiance to Rome—a ruler
who happened to be in Jerusalem, perhaps for Passover [vv.5–7].

Herod, who is described as more interested in watching a magic
show than looking for justice [v.8], gets nothing but silence from
Jesus in response to the questions asked of him and to the complaints from the Jewish authorities [vv.9–10]. We're told that Herod's disappointment was expressed not in anger, but in derision
and mockery.

These scenes may not seem to be about Jesus because the various
authorities—the officials from the Sanhedrin (see 22:66), Pilate, and
Herod—are depicted as obsessed with their own concerns: the Sanhedrin members with a conviction, Pilate with avoiding trouble,
and Herod with amusement. They're not interested in what Jesus
teaches about repentance, forgiveness, and the kingdom. So Jesus
has nothing to say as the power brokers of this world enjoy a bit of
farce [vv.11–12].

CONDEMNING THE INNOCENT [LK.23:13–25]

[13] *Pilate summoned the chief priests, other rulers, and the people who'd gathered.* [14] *He said, "You charged this man with inciting the people. I interrogated
him before you and found him not guilty of the charge.* [15] *Herod found the
same—he sent him back. He's done nothing to deserve death.* [16] *I'll have him
flogged and released."* [[17] *A note here about releasing a prisoner at Passover is
considered an editor's gloss.]* [18] *But everyone shouted, "Away with him. Give us
Barabbas."* [19] *He was a man who'd been charged with riot and murder in the city.*
[20] *Pilate spoke again, hoping to release Jesus.* [21] *But they shouted, "Crucify!
Crucify him!"* [22] *Again Pilate spoke: "What's he done wrong? I found no capital
guilt. I will flog and release him."* [23] *They shouted louder, demanding crucifixion.
Their voices won.* [24] *Pilate ruled that their demand could be granted.* [25] *He
released to them the one guilty of riot and murder, and he handed over Jesus to
do with as they wanted.*

The business gets messy here, but it gets done. Luke depicts Pilate as judging that there's no evidence Jesus had committed the capital crime of inciting unrest, and that Herod's lack of interest in the matter confirmed that judgment [vv.13–15]. But he says Pilate's offer to let Jesus off with a severe warning—a flogging [v.16]—didn't please the Jewish officials or the crowd (see 23:4). The crowd appears to have been persuaded to join the authorities in asking for the freedom of Barabbas [vv.16–19].

Luke tells us that, when Pilate tried again to enforce his decision [v.20], the crowd roared its disagreement with a clear call for death [v.21]. Although Luke seems to suggest Pilate didn't know he was losing this shouting match, its outcome is probably clear to any casual reader before it's described [vv.22–23].

According to Luke, Pilate must give in to a mob's demands in order to do the business of ruling without riot [v.24]. Once Jesus is released to the mob, they can go about the business they've set for themselves [v.25b]. (And Barabbas can presumably go back to whatever business occupied him before he'd been arrested [v.25a].) An injustice has been accomplished in a very businesslike way.

CARRYING OUT THE SENTENCE [LK.23:26–38]

26 As the mob led Jesus off, they seized Simon, a Cyrenian returning from the field, to carry the cross behind Jesus. 27 A large number of people followed him. When women lamented and wept, 28 Jesus turned and said, "Daughters of Jerusalem, don't weep for me. Weep for yourselves and your children. 29 Watch; days are coming when they'll say, 'Happy the barren, the wombs that never bore and the breasts that never nursed.' 30 They'll say to the mountains, 'Fall on us'; to the hills, 'Cover us' [Hos.10:8]. 31 If this is done when the wood is green, what will happen when it's dry?" 32 Now two other convicts were led along with him to be executed. 33 And when they reached "Skull Place," they crucified him with them on either side. [34 Words attributed to Jesus are added here in late texts.] Then they divided his clothes by casting lots. 35 The people stood and watched. The leaders laughed and said, "He saved others. Let him save himself if he's

God's anointed—the chosen one!" [36] *Soldiers also laughed. They went up and offered him some of their wine.* [37] *They said, "If you're the King of the Jews, save yourself."* [38] *There was an inscription above him: "This is the King of the Jews."*

Luke says the mob, given permission by Pilate (see above), rushed Jesus off to execution. By telling us the name and birthplace of a passing stranger who was forced to help speed things up [v.26], and by mentioning the reaction of some in the crowd [v.27], Luke emphasizes that this is a real event witnessed by various individuals with varying perspectives. He then describes Jesus pausing to tell his sympathizers they should grieve for themselves and for the offspring with whom they will not wish to share their future misery [vv.28–29]—a misery depicted in the Book of the Prophet Hosea in its description of the anguish of those who refuse to turn to God. Luke tells us Jesus used the image of tree growth to suggest the increase of woe that necessarily accumulates when one refuses to repent [v.31].

We can picture the mob catching up to a contingent of conscripted Roman soldiers (see below, v.36) who were escorting two others to the place of execution—a spot that may have gotten its name from its grisly association with death or from its rounded shape—where the three were set on crosses [vv.32–33]. While the executioners waited for death to occur, they could dispose of the prisoner's clothes [v.34]. There was little left to do but enjoy the irony of a healer forced to be hurt; the humiliation of someone who claimed to be loved by God—even considered by some to be God's Anointed One, the Messiah—exhibited as a helpless criminal [v.35]. According to Luke, the soldiers, who were most likely conscripts from other regions occupied by the empire, joined in the amusement with a mock-polite offer of wine, and laughed at the thought that such a woeful Jewish "king" could save anyone [vv.36–38].

ONE MORE ENCOUNTER BEFORE DYING; DEATH AND BURIAL [LK.23:39–56]

39 One criminal made fun: "If you're the Messiah, save yourself and us." 40 "Don't you fear God?" asked the other. "We're condemned men. 41 And we're here, rightly, for what we did. But this man did no wrong." 42 He asked Jesus, "Remember me when you enter your kingdom." 43 "O yes, indeed," said Jesus, "I say you'll be with me in Paradise today." 44 About noon, darkness fell on the land until about three. 44 The sun was obscured. The curtain in the Temple's sanctuary ripped in two. 46 Jesus called out, "Father, I give my spirit into your hands" [Ps.31:6], and died. 47 The commander who saw this praised God, saying, "This man was innocent." 48 The people who saw it returned home beating their breasts. 49 All his acquaintances and the women who'd followed him also saw what happened. 50 Now, there was a member of the Sanhedrin who was named Joseph. He was good and just. 51 A Jew from Arimathea, who longed for the kingdom, he'd had no part in the plot. 52 He went and obtained Pilate's permission to take the body of Jesus away. 53 He took it down, wrapped it in linen, and laid it a new, rock-hewn tomb. 54 It was the day after the Passover, and a preparation day for a Sabbath. 55 Some women who had accompanied Jesus followed Joseph to see where the body was laid. 56 They left to mix spices and ointments, then observed the Sabbath command to rest.

—————

Above, Luke depicted the plotting leaders and the mob in a rush to rid themselves of Jesus. But Jesus is neither rushed nor deterred from teaching what he has taught from the beginning: the joy of turning to the Lord—repentance (see 4:17–21). Luke just pictured him pausing to speak to women about repentance; and here he describes Jesus enjoying a conversation—and a promise—about the joys of paradise with an unlikely penitent [vv.39–43]. The darkening of the sun and unveiling of the sanctuary reported by Luke can be read as symbolic, but they're also reminders that the world isn't under human control [vv.44–45]. Then Luke describes Jesus—as he has described him throughout the Gospel—acknowledging his human weakness by entrusting himself to the strength of God, and doing so with words learned from a Psalm [v.46]. As Luke describes it, a surprising witness at this improbable moment recognized Jesus' act of dying as a reason to thank God [v.47], and the individuals who'd acted as a mob began to be moved by repentance [v.48]. Meanwhile, Jesus' followers waited and watched [v.49].

According to Luke, one of the Sanhedrin (see 22:66) who hadn't plotted against Jesus used his clout and means to give Jesus a respectful burial [vv.50–53]. When Luke tells us this day of execution was before a Sabbath [v.54], he reveals why the plotters may have been in such a hurry—their religious convictions would keep them from doing any business on a Sabbath—and why the women who were anxious to give Jesus' corpse the traditional anointing had time only to make the mixture, not to use it [vv.55–56]. They must wait to return on the third day.

TWENTY-FOUR

Jesus, Risen, Preaches Repentance, Then Is Taken into Heaven

DISCIPLES CAN'T FIND JESUS [LK.24:1–12]

¹ Very early, on the first day of the week, the women took their spices to the tomb. ² They found the stone rolled away from the tomb's entrance. ³ They went in, but didn't find the body of the Lord Jesus. ⁴ In their bewilderment, imagine, two men in radiant clothing appeared to them. ⁵ They crouched in terror. The men said, "Why seek the living one among the dead? ⁶ He isn't here. He's raised. Remember what he told you while in Galilee. ⁷ 'The Son of Man must be given to sinners, crucified, and rise on the third day.'" ⁸ They remembered these words of his [see 9:22]. ⁹ Then they returned from the tomb and told all this to the eleven and everyone else. ¹⁰ And they—that is, Mary Magdalene, Joanna, Mary the mother of James, and others—kept repeating it to the apostles. ¹¹ But their story seemed silly. The others didn't believe them. ¹² But Peter got up and ran to the tomb. Bending to look in, he saw burial cloths by themselves. He went away wondering what had happened.

Luke says the women who had to wait until the conclusion of the Sabbath before they could return to the tomb on the third day went first thing as the new week began [v.1]. But they didn't find what they expected [vv.2–3]. Although Luke describes the appearance of the strangers as extraordinary, he reports that their words were simple: a reminder to the women of Jesus' words about betrayal, death, and rising [vv.4–7]. Then, says Luke, the women did remember [v.8]. Notice that Luke is telling us that they needed—and received—supernatural help to realize they'd been pursuing expectations that were the opposite of what Jesus told them to expect—they were expecting to find a dead body; Jesus had told them to expect his rising.

Suddenly, according to Luke, the women were so excited by their new expectation that they couldn't help telling and retelling the events that had led to this change [vv.9–10]. Luke doesn't say why he identifies some characters by name, some by their role (the remaining eleven apostles) and some generally ("others"), but the effect suggests a rather confused crowd of followers, gathered in some temporary lodging (or in hiding; or still on Mt. Olives?) in a city where their teacher had been executed. According to Luke, the women's newfound excitement added to the confusion [v.11] and provoked Peter to investigate matters for himself—an investigation that, according to Luke, didn't bring him much closer to believing Jesus' assurance that he would rise from the dead [v.12].

JESUS TEACHES TWO FLEEING DISCIPLES ABOUT TRUST
[LK.24:13–31]

[13] *That day, two disciples headed home to Emmaus, some miles from Jerusalem.* [14] *On the way, they talked about all that had happened.* [15] *As they spoke and argued, Jesus came up and walked with them.* [16] *But their eyes were clouded and they didn't recognize him.* [17] *"What've you been talking about as you walk along?" They stopped and stared.* [18] *One of them, Cleopas, asked, "Are you the only visitor to Jerusalem ignorant of what happened there?"* [19] *"What?" said Jesus. They said, "What happened to Jesus of Nazareth! He was a prophet whose works and words were powerful before God and all the people.* [20] *Our chief priests and leaders handed him over to be condemned to death on a cross.* [21] *We'd hoped he would be the one to redeem Israel. It's the third day since it*

happened. [22] *Some of the women in the group who were at the tomb this morning bewildered us.* [23] *They didn't find his body. They came and said angels had told them he was alive.* [24] *Others went and saw the tomb as the women described it. But they didn't see him."* [25] *"What dull hearts!" he said. "You're so slow to believe all that the prophets said.* [26] *Did you think the Messiah wouldn't have to suffer such things to enter glory?"* [27] *Then, starting with Moses, he showed how scripture spoke of him.* [28] *As they approached Emmaus, he seemed ready to go on.* [29] *But they said, "Come home with us. It's late. The day's over." So, he stayed.* [30] *At table with them, he took bread, said the blessing, broke it, and gave it to them.* [31] *Their eyes cleared, and they recognized him. And he disappeared.*

———◦∞◦———

Luke has told us people followed Jesus from many towns. Now he describes two returning home [v.13]—disappointment clouding their eyes [vv.14–16]. This description is wry rather than solemn as Jesus joins their woeful conversation and plays along with their worries [vv.17–19a]. Luke lets these disciples detail their disillusionment [vv.19b–24] and tells us Jesus nudged them—with a sharp elbow—to reconsider their ideas about struggling, suffering, and dying [vv.25–26]. Then, perhaps for the first time, they listened to what scripture has to say about the difference between God's view of suffering and ours. Whether or not Jesus mentioned the ambitions of Adam and Eve or the whining of Job, we're to assume he gave them a grand tour of scripture's many examples of how foolishly we assume we know how life is supposed to work [v.27].

After an invitation to visit [vv.28–29], Luke says Jesus did what he'd done before with his disciples—he gave thanks to God as he broke the bread [v.30]. In this simple act, the disciples again saw Jesus doing what he'd tried to teach them to do: in all things, turn trustingly to God, and give thanks [v.31].

Chapter 24

JESUS CONFRONTS THE DOUBTS OF HIS DISCIPLES
[LK.24:32–43]

³² In Emmaus, the two disciples said, "Weren't our hearts aflame when he opened scripture to us on the way!" ³³ They got right up and went back to Jerusalem—to the group of eleven and others, ³⁴ who told them, "The Lord is really raised! He appeared to Simon!" ³⁵ The two spoke of their journey, and how they saw him in the breaking of the bread. ³⁶ As they spoke, Jesus stood there with them and said, "Peace be with you." ³⁷ Startled, they all feared they were seeing a ghost. ³⁸ He said, "Why are you troubled? Why do doubts flood your hearts? ³⁹ Look at my hands and feet. I'm me. Touch and see. A ghost has no flesh and bones." ⁴⁰ He showed them his hands and feet. ⁴¹ Joyful but confused, they couldn't believe him. He asked, "Have you anything to eat?" ⁴² They gave him a piece of broiled fish. ⁴³ He took it and ate it there.

Luke describes intense and fluctuating emotions provoked by Jesus' appearances to his disciples. We hear that the two from Emmaus realized Jesus' review of scripture (see 24:27) had stirred their hearts as well as their minds [v.32]. Like the women who'd listened to the angels (see 24:9), these two disciples hurried to bring their fresh excitement back to the group—where they found the others in a similar state of agitation [vv.33–35].

Suddenly, says Luke, they were all filled with fear, despite Jesus' invitation to be at peace [vv.36–37]. We can assume that, like all the rest in the group, the two who'd just returned from their encounter with Jesus—and even Simon, perhaps—found it easier to suppose they were being visited by a ghost rather than the teacher who'd told them he would rise from the dead. Luke says Jesus asked them to notice the doubts that were bedeviling them [v.38]. Then he helped them to reflect on what they actually saw: him [v.39]. Then, says Luke, Jesus spoke like someone who tries to soothe a child who's had a bad dream—saying, "Look, no ghosts!" as he waggles his hands and feet [v.40]. But he was apparently unable to calm the storm of their conflicting hopes and doubts [v.41a]. According to

Luke, Jesus tried something else to help them stop fixating on their uncertainty and fear. To help them see the truth of what was before them, he ate some fish [vv.41b–43].

JESUS PROCLAIMS HIS MESSAGE ONCE MORE; HE IS TAKEN UP TO HEAVEN [LK.24:44–53]

⁴⁴ Jesus continued to speak to his disciples: "The words I spoke to you were to show how truly the Law of Moses, the prophets, and the Psalms wrote of me." ⁴⁵ Then he opened their minds that they might understand the scriptures. ⁴⁶ "So, it's been written: the Messiah will suffer, and rise from the dead the third day; ⁴⁷ and repentance and forgiveness of sins will be preached in his name to all nations, starting in Jerusalem. ⁴⁸ You're the witnesses of these things. ⁴⁹ Wait and watch; I will send my Father's promise [of the Spirit]. Stay in the city until you receive its power." ⁵⁰ He then walked with them to Bethany. There, he lifted his arms in blessing. ⁵¹ As he blessed them, he was parted from them—carried up to heaven. ⁵² They worshiped him. They went back to Jerusalem with great joy. ⁵³ They were always in the Temple, praising God.

―――☙☙☙――――

The reader assumes that Jesus' attempts to calm his disciples (see above) finally worked. Luke depicts Jesus explaining to an attentive audience the purpose of all his lessons: to help them see that God's promise—as it's expressed in the Covenant, in the Law of Moses, in the reminders of the prophets, and in the prayerful Psalms—is fulfilled in him [v.44]. With his words and deeds still fresh in their memories, Jesus seemed able to help them see how perfectly he had trusted everything that scripture taught: that is, its lessons about struggling, suffering, and learning to let God have his way, as well as its call to invite others to taste the delights of turning to God, repenting one's selfish ways, and finding forgiveness [vv.45–47].

Luke tells us Jesus reminded the disciples that they'd seen him embody and live out the lessons taught by scripture [v.48], and that now they should wait for him to fill them with God's own Spirit and power—the same Spirit and power possessed by Jesus [v.49].

According to Luke, Jesus made a parting gesture—a benediction that signaled his intention to keep his promise to bless them with power [vv.50–51]. Luke describes the disciples sharing an awareness that their relationship with Jesus had deepened from disciple to worshipful devotee—a devotee who follows Jesus' example by giving joyful thanks to God [v.52]. They obeyed his command to wait for the Spirit in the city. Like Anna (see 2:37), they spent their time in the Temple, blessing God—and waiting [v.53].

Index

About the Author

Paul J. McCarren, SJ, works at Loyola Retreat House and at St. Ignatius Church, both in Maryland, while continuing to write Simple Guides to the Bible. A Jesuit priest, he has spent many years in both parish and campus ministry.